GW01087123

Life, Love and High Marks

Other great books to get your hands on

Anita Naik:
Am I Normal?
Families: can't live with them, can't live without them!
Is this Love?
The 'Just Seventeen' Quiz Book

Adele Lovell:
The Just Seventeen Guide to being Gorgeous

Helen Benedict:
Stand up for Yourself!

Victoria McCarthy:
Don't just sit there — Get a Life!

Charlotte Owen:
Everything you wanted to know about periods ...
but didn't like to ask!

LIFE, LOVE AND HIGH MARKS

By
Kate Brookes

**Illustrations by
Christine Roche**

Hodder
Children's
Books

a division of Hodder Headline

HODDER CHILDREN'S BOOKS IMPRINTS

Text © Kate Brookes 1997
Illustrations © Christine Roche 1997

First published in 1997 by Hodder Children's Books

Edited by Kay Barnham
Designed by Karen Donald @ Wilson Design Associates

10 9 8 7 6 5 4 3 2 1

A catalogue record for this book is available from the British Library.

ISBN 0 340 67094 0

Hodder Children's Books
A division of Hodder Headline
338 Euston Road
London NW1 3BH

Printed and bound by
The Guernsey Press Co. Ltd, Vale, Guernsey, Channel Islands

Contents

All About Kate

Long before Kate put her dab hand to writing, she was an over-worked, under-paid and suffering student. Just saying the word 'student' within earshot of Kate used to make her go all pale and shivery. School days were not dream days for this lass. But that changed when she met the Tank-topped Professor. He gave her a handle on how to cope with school day doldrums. He said you've got to have a goal. Kate was off at a fast trot (a gallop would have been well out of character) to get control of her life, get the man of her dreams, get out more often and get high marks. And she almost did it!

Total control of her life has sort of eluded her, what with two children, a cat, two gerbils and absolutely no idea of when the dustmen come. But – and it's a BIG but – she did get the man of her (and all her mates') dreams, had a social life that gossip columnists are still writing about AND she flew through her exams with the greatest of sleaze ... I mean, ease.

Introduction

⇒ THE GETTING ⇒ OF SASS

Comprehensive school, we are told, is a heavy number. Gone are the idylls of middle or primary school where you were giants among the little people, and the teachers came to you. Gone are the **long** hours in the playground, and short ones in the library. Now it's homework, tests, self-initiative, homework, private study, coursework, even more homework, deadlines, and hair-raising runs from classroom to classroom (gnaw fingernails nervously). And all the while the shadow of curriculum tests, GCSEs and Standard Grades loom menacingly from above (no fingernails left, starting on toe-nails). And who said *Point Horror* isn't real?

But school doesn't have to be a battlefield for your brain. All you've got to do is get a grip on some stonkingly-wicked school survival skills. And guess what? The value-packed paperback that you have clenched in your hands is full to bursting with just such wickedness. Take heed of the down-to-earth advice and you can forget:

- ➡ Sleepless nights spent tossing and turning in your bed trying to think of a plausible excuse why your homework hasn't been done in time;
- ➡ Breaking out in a cold sweat when teachers spring a surprise test on you;
- ➡ Going blank during an exam;
- ➡ Spending your high school life locked behind closed doors, socially dormant with your head in a book;
- ➡ Being given a hard time by your parents, teachers and mates;
- ➡ Being unable to spell accommodation, parliament and sincerely.

Yeah, but what's the catch, you ask. There isn't one. Skating through comprehensive school is dead simple when you've got a cunningly stupendous plan that helps you polish up your class act, finish homework in a flash, and wow your teachers.

All you need is The Megatastic Grand Plan (see Chapter One), the nous to give teachers and examiners what they want, the way to remember things, and most importantly, the wisdom to decide when it's time to bust out and party, or dream of being loofahed by Boyzone. See, it's a doddle.

Sad thing is that no-one teaches SASS (Surviving At School Skills). Parents think the instructions for SASS are sewn into the hem of your uniform, and teachers, poor dears, just run out of huff and puff before they can tell you. What with nine or ten subjects to force-feed into the minds of a thousand or so kids, form meetings, after-school stuff, sweat sessions on the playing field, assignments to mark, and all that curriculum paperwork to file, there just ain't enough hours in the day for teachers to let you in on the secrets that can turn high school hell into heaven.

From the wading pool of primary school you're suddenly pushed into the deep end of the diving pool and expected to swim – not fair! No wonder you want to bury your head in a bucket of sand when you get home from school.

Well, forget the ostrich act and kiss goodbye to brain strain. The good life awaits.

Homework Quiz

First let's get a handle on your attitude to school, homework, teachers and peanut butter sandwiches. Think of this quick quiz as an RoA – a Record of Attitude – where you can be as up-front and honest as you like. There are no smiley badges for getting correct answers, and no one fails.

FIRST DAY BACK AT SCHOOL ARE YOU
A) full of breathless anticipation at the exciting challenges ahead?
B) scared out of your wits and about to throw up?
C) wishing you were at home polishing the spokes on your bike?

THE TEACHER OF YOUR NIGHTMARES SETS YOU A TONNE OF HOMEWORK DUE THE NEXT DAY, DO YOU
A) gather all your courage together and tell your teacher that it would be very difficult to do justice to this assignment with such a short deadline? (Very smooth. I'm impressed.)
B) accept that it's your lot and stay up all night to finish it?
C) spend three hours on the phone after school telling your mates the teacher is off his/her rocker if he/she thinks you're going to do it?

AT THE END OF EACH CLASS DO YOU
A) make sure you recall all the crucial stuff covered in the lesson?
B) pray that an act of God will close the school before the next bell?
C) race out so fast your trainers burn rubber?

A MEGA-MAJOR PROJECT HAS BEEN SET, DO YOU
A) recruit a couple of friends and delegate the work?
B) prepare for a long, lonely siege and martyr yourself on the pyre of learning?
C) forget about it until the night before?

ALL YOUR FRIENDS ARE DOING GERMAN, DO YOU
A) stick to your plan to do French?
B) tag along even though you really want to do French?
C) go to German because you don't care what you study?

DO YOU THINK TEACHERS AND EXAMINERS ARE OUT TO GET YOU?
A) Nope.
B) Of course. Exams and stuff are not meant to be easy.
C) They can try, but you'll give them hell first.

YOU GET BOTTOM OF THE BARREL MARKS ON A TEST, DO YOU
A) get upset for a while and then try to work out what went wrong?
B) decide that you'll never do well in that subject, so you may as well forget about it?
C) congratulate yourself on being consistent?

WHAT DOES EATING PEANUT SANDWICHES SAY ABOUT A PERSON?
A) Pardon?
B) Don't know. Will it be in the exams?
C) Crunchy or smooth?

On the basis of how you answered these questions, see which description fits you.

TYPE A: WAY TO GO!

"I think I'm a pretty good student because I know what I want to do with my life, and I know that the teachers are there to help. But if they're not doing a good job or are expecting way too much, then I can't afford to ignore it or struggle to keep up on my own. I try to get all my homework completed and make sure it's presentable. Sometimes school is pretty terrifying – the work is getting harder and my parents are breathing down my neck – but I still like it most of the time."

TYPE B: YOU'VE GOT TO LEARN TO CHILL OUT.

"I worry about school and my work all the time, and I don't care how long it takes me to do everything, the important thing is that I finish it. It's no use complaining. I'm sure

others have tried and failed. Anyway, teachers will come down on you like a tonne of bricks if they think you're talking about them to the head teacher or someone. School isn't meant to be a picnic, and when I do badly at something that's just the way it's meant to be. I like to stick to my friends at school, it makes me feel safe."

TYPE C: CAN I INTEREST YOU IN AN ATTITUDE CHANGE?

"School is evil. I do the minimum and spend my time hanging around with my mates and seeing My Man. Teachers are a pain but what else can you expect – they're not paid to be your bosom buddies. I don't do my homework if I can get away with it, and exams are a joke. They don't count for anything anyway, so why worry about them? I can't wait till I can leave school and get a job."

Chapter

One

THE MEGATASTIC GRAND PLAN

- Everything about: making the most of your precious time
○ Nothing about: being a boffin

The secret in having it all – great life, rave results, and stress-free school days – lies in, and I hesitate to say it, a bit of planning. This is a dull word used by dull people who have totally lost it when it comes to spontaneity. These peeps have given planning a bad name.

They think that planning is getting their knickers together for the coming week, coordinating them with their outfit (as if anyone's going to notice) and labelling them. Wrong! This is not planning, it's a sign that they should get out more. Then there are the drones who organize their cassettes using the Dewey Decimal System. Why would you do it unless you were desperately looking for something, anything, to do? And everyone knows someone who colour codes their school kit so that they can tell a maths book from a pair of PE shorts. Is this good planning? No, it's time for an eye test. These guys plan because it's the only – and I mean only – way they get their kicks.

Real planning is a kit of cunningly stupendous tactics that help you find the slickest route through the everyday stuff, like homework and revision, so that you can get on with living. The Megatastic Grand Plan makes it easy for you to do everything you want, when you want to do it, and to do it in your own sassy style. It puts you in control.

Have I got your attention, dudettes? Good, so stick with me, there's only one more thing to take on board before The Megatastic Grand Plan is all yours. Putting together your living-and-loving-it scheme requires a teeny bit of work.

If you wanted to have a party, you wouldn't expect the party people to roll up, for the music to be blaring and a spread of food laid out unless you did some organizing. You've got to decide when and where the party will be and then tell your pals about it. You've got to rally help in order to make the munchies and wire up the suburb-shaking speakers. Of course, you could forget the organizing and stay at home by yourself, but that would be too sad. Sob, sob, sniffle, sniffle, wipe nose on shirt sleeve.

The same sort of planning is needed if you want to get great marks and have a life. Oh, but what am I saying? For all I know you could already have the game sussed and sorted. You might have started filling in your homework diary and study planner, stocked up on must-have stationery bits, and implored your family to buy you a whole heap of new books. If so, close this book carefully, while shaking out the toast crumbs, and return it to the bookshop. You don't need this book, you need a medal.

(Dear Reader, I don't know where Kate comes off saying things like that. This book is more than just a buying guide for fluorescent paper clips. What about all the stuff on writing essays, coping with exams, and all those dead quick ways of remembering things? Forget about going to the bookshop. Read on. The Editor.

PS.You can never get all the toast crumbs out.)

The Megatastic Grand Plan

Assuming that you have made it out of bed, into a uniform, on to a bus and through the gates without incident, these are the four basic tricks to surviving and thriving at school.

- Go to lessons
- Do your homework
- Keep up with revision
- Be ready for tests and exams

Dead simple IF you do it regularly. Big pain if you don't. "So how do you do it, Kate? What's the plan?"

STEP 1: Seeing into the future

You don't need Mystic Meg, crystal balls or tea leaves to tell you your future. All you need is a homework diary and a year planner. With accuracy unknown to the world of astrology you will know weeks, if not months, in advance when an assignment is due, or a test or party is coming your way. With a diary there's no chance of foul interplanetary influences making you miss deadlines or days of frolic.

If you haven't got a year planner, draw one yourself! Leave enough room for three months and make three photocopies to cover all twelve months, or you can race out to 'We Have Stationery' and buy a ready-made poster-sized one. While you're there pick up anything else you need for your Homework Heaven (see page 28). I'll give you half an hour to get yourself fixed. In the meantime I'm going to save a site of great archeological significance from the bulldozer of progress.

GOING FOR THE STARS?? GET REAL, girl - GET YOURSELF A DIARY!

DATES WITH DESTINY

Once you've got the goods, fill in your homework diary and year planner with the dates of tests and exams, and the deadlines for any mega projects. One week before these dates write '1 week until...'. In an ideal world, you would hope to have everything finished or revised by that date. But the world isn't perfect (if it was, I would be dating Keanu and Jared Leto), so don't get hot and bothered if all doesn't go according to plan. Remember, you've still got a week to go. Cunning, eh?

Then mark on your diary and planner those days when you have after-school activities. Also jot down things like Inset Days, school trips and sports days. Each in their own way has an effect (usually good) on the amount of homework you'll get that night.

Some teachers always give homework on a particular day and want it finished by a set day the following week. If so, you can write these into your homework diary as well.

Now for the crucial stuff of which life is made: the good times. Use your homework book and planner as a social diary as well. Hot date Saturday – put it down. Family outing Sunday – write in it. A must-see film on Tuesday – put it in your diary. No good planning to start a geography assignment on Wednesday when there's an el cheapo session at the ice rink.

STEP 2: Putting on a star class performance

If you play your cards right in class, you'll be halfway to cutting your homework and revision down to size. To find out all about classroom class, flick to Chapter Three.

STEP 3: Raid the fridge

Every afternoon after school raid the fridge. You've got to keep your energy up, and give your parents something to moan about. Because from this day on, baby, they won't be moaning about homework or anything else. They'll see you've got everything under control.

STEP 4: Hitting the trail for Homework Heaven

After you have munched out, head to your Homework Heaven (see Chapter Two for decorating tips) and give yourself about half an hour to go over your notes from school

GOT TO GIVE THEM SOMETHING TO MOAN ABOUT – N'EST-CE PAS?

that day. Make sure you understand what you've written, and get the drift of hand-outs.

If there are any questions about a particular class or set of notes, write them down in your homework diary and raise them with the teacher the next day. Stick one of those sticky yellow thingummies to your notes, and only remove it when you know your notes are complete.

Then, using all the ideas in Notable Notes (page 47) jazz up your notes to make them truly outstanding and totally memorable. Rewrite hand-outs in your own words.

"Why would I want to do that for Pete's sake?"

Because them-in-the-know say that 'transforming' – putting the teacher's mutterings into your own words – is THE way of learning and remembering. If you don't give class notes, hand-outs and research notes the make-over, they all go in one ear and out the other. Capish?

The next thing to do is your homework. (Don't all shout hooray at once.) I know homework is the biggest drag this side of Lily Savage, but there is good news. If you use all the tricks in Chapter Five you'll be off the hard shoulder of homework hell at warp speed.

You can sadly assume that there will be some homework every night. Some teachers will tell you how long a piece of homework should take, but if they haven't, ask them. You've got better things to do than spend two hours on an assignment that was intended to take 20 minutes. But if the teach is not forthcoming, make sure you give yourself lots of time. Better to finish before you expect (and in time to catch up on events at the Vic), than to be constantly running out of time, working up a lather and holding work over until the next night.

STEP 5: Kiss cramming goodbye
(no tears needed)

Pick two consecutive nights during the week (and mark them on your year planner ... now!) when you know that the following will be in short supply: homework, good telly, leg hair to wax and rave happenings. On these nights you can get on top of big projects and assignments, or some reading.

No homework? No projects? No reading? Then go party, Cinders, but be back in time to sweep out the fireplace and do a spot of revision.

"Revision, you've got to be joking. I haven't got a test for weeks. I'm not doing any studying and that's that!"

OK, so leave it until the day before the test. See if I care when you stay up all night, get into a panic because you suddenly realize that you didn't understand all that stuff about glaciation, and it's too late to call your friends. See if I care when you drag yourself into school after only a couple of hours' sleep, looking like something that's been dragged through a hedge backwards. And don't come running to me looking for sympathy and a shoulder to cry on when you bum the test.

STEP 6: The Pizza Theory

On the remaining free evenings during the work-a-day week, allocate two subjects for revision and mark them on your year planner. As little as 15–20 minutes of revision for each subject a night is going to show in your results. As you get closer to tests and exams, increase your revision time. And when will that be? Look in your diary and planner and find out.

Choose two contrasting subjects, for example history and CDT, or English and maths, to study each evening. By the end of a two-week period you will have revised the work in every subject to date. Go on, and revel in smug satisfaction.

"But what about my pizza?" It's coming up. The Pizza Theory is the gourmet way of learning, so wash your hands and don your pinny for some food technology.

PIZZA TO GO	LEARNING A-GO-GO
Flour, water, yeast for dough	*Everything you learn at school*
Tomato paste	*Homework*
Mozzarella	*Big projects*
Toppings of your choice	*Revision*
Thoroughly mix ingredients for dough.	***Read your class notes and make them memorable by transforming them.***
Knead and roll dough until it is good and smooth.	*Go over your notes until you understand them.*
Allow dough to rest.	***To keep yourself in top form don't work for long periods without a break.***
Shape dough into pizza pan.	*Put class notes and other work into subject files or workbooks.*
Evenly spread tomato paste over pizza.	***Do your homework regularly.***
Sprinkle on mozzarella.	*Don't forget to do long-term projects and reading a couple of nights a week.*
Cover with toppings.	***Revise a couple of subjects each night.***
Bake slowly.	*Give yourself time to learn, you'll burn out if you cram.*

The proof of the cooking is in the eating, or should it be that the proof of the work is in your results?

How's that for good value from a book? You've already had a pizza and been given a tour of The Megatastic Grand Plan, and we're only up to page 21. Now brew up your favourite bevvy, curl up cosy-like on a comfortable couch and learn how to be kind to yourself.

Kindness that counts

BE FLEXIBLE

Just because you don't do your homework or revision one day, doesn't mean that the whole plan has to be flushed down the toilet. All you have to do is a little bit of shuffling. What you don't do one day can be done the next or over the weekend. That's the charm in having a plan that gives you heaps of time in which to do things – there's never a panic because nothing is left to the last minute.

DON'T FORGET THE BIG TICK

To keep tabs on your super-slick progress through the slog of school work, give yourself The Big Tick (not the sort you find on a dog) when a subject is done, a deadline met, homework completed, a class prepared or notes sorted.

Teachers have been using the big tick since the Boy King, Tutankhamun, went to Scribal School Comprehensive – because it works. There's nothing more satisfying (gross exaggeration here) than seeing a page covered with 'done it, been there, read the book, bought the T-shirt' ticks.

PILE ON THE PRAISE AND REWARDS

When you've done well, lash out on self-praise (if you can get your parents to join in all the better) and pile on the rewards (if you can get your parents to pay for them, better still).

SHARE THE PLEASURE, SHARE THE PAIN

You've lots to do and heaps on your mind because you're making your way through both the toughest and the best years of your life. There's this school lark to contend with, bad hair days to conquer, careers to suss, and luurve relationships to develop. You're a busy person, so don't carry the burden alone. Get your family and friends involved.

MAKE WAY FOR PRIVATE PASSIONS

Let's say you've got a burning desire to do ballroom dancing (strictly for fun, of course) and classes run on a Wednesday night. Great, so just move the revision subjects from Wednesday evening to a set time over the weekend. But it's hard over the weekend: you want to do things, your parents want you to go out with them, there are chores to be done, and you've got a part-time job.

Get together with your best friends and agree that for a couple of hours over the weekend (two short sessions are better than one loooong bout of book-bashing) you are all incommunicado –

no phone calls, no outings, no nothing. In this way you know that you are all suffering together. Then tell your parents that on no account are they to hassle you for anything during that set time. And if you've got no work to do, then the time's your own. Way to go!

Other ways of sharing the pleasure and pain: find a study buddy who's ace in the subjects you're not; get your family to proof your essays and give you spot tests; share the library run with someone; and divvy up the house chores with a sibling.

STOP THE GUILT TRIPS

Just because you didn't get to tick everything, and you didn't get 'PERFECT' scrawled at the bottom at your homework, there's no need to feel bad. Inevitably, a case of the guilts erodes your self-confidence and causes your positive attitude to take a dive. Anyway, just think of all the time you're going to waste meandering around the house moaning and beating yourself with a wire brush. It's not worth it. Accept that you had a so-so day, but that it's not the end of the world. To knock problems down to size see page 37.

WORK-FREE ZONE

Never work when you're sick, tired or depressed. Not only will your work suffer, you won't help yourself get better.

The Distracting Demons

Dear Kate,

"The Megatastic Grand Plan and everything else sounds just dandy, but something or someone always gets in the way. What do I do?"

Yours truly,

Highly Distracted.

In every home there lurk distracting demons (DDs) who entice us away from what we really want to do. They feed on our time, and the more time we give them, the bigger they get. The problem with DDs is that they can assume many forms. One minute they're a soap opera on the TV, the next they appear as irresistible nibbles In the fridge. Some have even been known to take on the characteristics of an interesting conversation with a younger brother. I know, it's unbelievable.

Following is a list of some of the most commonly encountered distracting demons. Be on your guard, it's your time they want.

THE FOOD DEMON

You've just got yourself ready to do some homework and turned to page 10 of your science book, when all of a sudden you have the urge to eat. It's not that you're hungry (you've just polished off a loaf of bread and three apples), the demons are making you delay. Anything, even a week-old slice of pizza is better than tackling this assignment. The DD has lured you to the 'fridge where you will spend the next half hour foraging. Once the demon knows your weakness, it will attack again.

Beating the demon: have a basket of fruit and healthy nibbles on your desk.

THE TELEPHONE DEMON

Demons work long-distance by making your friends call you, and in doing so have made you and your mate lose valuable time. Granted you had a terrific gossip, but what you have to remember is that all the time you're chatting, the distracting demon is chuckling with delight.

Giving DD the engaged signal: tell your family that you don't want to speak to friends (even though it's good to talk) for the next hour or so, and ask them to take messages. Turn down the bell on the phone so that you can't hear it or have the phone moved completely out of earshot.

THE TV DEMON

This is possibly the most effective of all distractions because it's out of your control. It's not like you can just slap a total ban on the TV while you're studying – other members of your family might be a little stroppy if deprived of *Top of the Pops*. This is one of the reasons why the television demon is so successful. The other is that even three-metre-thick, lead-lined walls will not stop the melodious theme tune of *Neighbours* reaching your eardrums and breaking your concentration. Before you know it, you've gone walkabout and are standing in front of Ramsey Street. Gotcha, says the demon.

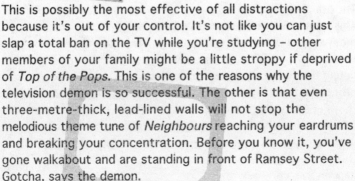

DEMON DEMON DEMON

Giving it the flick: first, ask your family to turn the TV down real quiet, then buy yourself a pair of ear muffs (also worth their weight in gold when it comes to not hearing your mum ask you to do the washing up). A second line of defence is to use the TV as a reward. Decide which programmes are in the 'must watch' category, but agree with yourself (and this shouldn't be hard) that you can't watch them until you've done your French irregular verbs, sorted out your notes and done a research hit-list for a project. This sort of planning really gets up the demon's nose.

THE POP-IN DEMON

What can you do when the demon makes your friends pop in for a goss? I mean, you can't shut the door on your mates, nor can you pretend you're not at home or have a deadly infectious disease. (That game's blown when you turn up the next day at school.) The other problem is that you quite like having your mates around and enjoy spending some quality couch time together.

Getting the demon to pop-off: tell your friends that you like to chill-out for a couple of hours when you get home from school and could they pop-around a bit later. If you can't resist a good-chin wag, you'll just have to be flexible with your diary and planner. But be on your guard, this demon does not give up without a fight.

THE DEMON THAT IS YOU

This demon is really subversive because he makes you do the most extraordinary things. You'll get the uncontrollable urge to debate the CFC/ozone issue with your mum, or talk to your young brother about his bug collection. Ordinarily there is everything to be said for having a chat with your family – it's a good thing, but why does it happen the night before a test? Because the demons make it happen.

Silencing the demon: the very instant you're hit by a case of the chats, start talking to yourself, preferably about the topic you're studying. I know such behaviour is medically certifiable, but it works. Firstly you've satisfied the need to make your chin go up and down, and secondly, by talking yourself through a difficult topic, you've learnt something.

SUMMARY:

1. Having a homework and study plan puts you in control.

2. Lesson time, homework and revision are all tied together. (There will be no pizza of success unless you have all the ingredients.)

3. Doing everything regularly will result in cramming becoming dodo-like – extinct.

4. You're one mighty fine example of the species, so treat yourself with a little tenderness.

5. The distracting demons are out there – don't let them get you.

Chapter Two

DO-IT-YOURSELF HOMEWORK HEAVEN

- Everything about: desk-top must-haves and attitude make-overs
- Nothing about: being a wuss

What do you call Homework Heaven? (Not having any is NOT the answer I'm looking for.) Is it a nook at the top of the stairs or maybe a desk in your room? Have you reserved a cosy spot in the local library or do you spread out on the carpet in front of a radiator? When it comes to the crunch, as the following list of luminary luvvies shows, where you do your work isn't nearly as important as doing it.

WELL, if it's good enough for DARWIN....

- Benjamin Disraeli, British Prime Minister (1874–80) could only write when wearing top hat and tails. And if you think you've found a new angle on sleaze, forget it. Disraeli wore trousers as well.
- Roald Dahl penned his books in a potting shed.
- French good egg and all-round friend of the Revolutionary masses Jean-Paul Marat, did much of his work in the bath.
- Impressionist painter Claude Monet couldn't get enough of the great outdoors, so he rigged up his studio in the middle of a lake.
- Charles Darwin wrote *The Origin of the Species* while propped up in bed.
- When these bods created their Homework Heavens, some of them plumped for pillows, others plumped for plumbing. So what does it take to make a Homework Heaven?

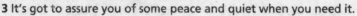

1 It's got to be comfortable.

2 It must motivate and inspire you.

3 It's got to assure you of some peace and quiet when you need it.

4 It must make the task of doing your homework unbelievably enjoyable. OK, so I might have overstated the joyous bit, but being somewhere you like has got to make the job easier. Agree?

The hardwear

The big arguments for having a desk are that it gets you used to exam-type conditions, that everything is within reach (avoids long walkabouts to find a ruler and dictionary) and stops your parents hassling you.

● The other plus of having your own special Homework Heaven is that your brain will associate it with studying and will slip into study gear as you slide behind the desk. It also means that when you leave Homework Heaven, you are leaving work behind and stepping into living mode.

● A good work area needs to be evenly lit (full spectrum daylight bulbs are the best). Desk lamps which throw lots of light on to the page but leave the rest of the room in semi-darkness are bad news. They cause what the peeper professionals refer to as 'visual fatigue'. In other words, your eyes get dead pooped.

● Wherever you set yourself up needs to be well-ventilated and not too warm. Anything warmer than 21°C (get out your thermometer) will put you to sleep.

GET PERSONAL

Give your Homework Heaven the personal touch. Blu Tack the walls with inspiring, but not wildly distracting*, posters and give it some plant life. Go overboard on stationery (see page 32) and have a tucker tub within reach. Oh yeah, and by the way, make sure the chair is comfortable. (Deep philosophical moment on the way.) The brain can only retain what the bottom can sustain! Put a couple of your most treasured collectables on your desk. When you're really stuck for an answer glance fondly at them and recall the good times they are associated with.

* Wildly distracting posters include: popping pec shots of Christian Slater, any Sloggi ad, and Gazza close-ups (Yuk!).

This little mental stroll in the park might just be the diversion your mind needs in order to free up the answer lurking deep inside your brain. A friend of mine used to keep a nodding dog on her desk (a priceless bit of tat she won at a fair) and when she got stuck on something, she used to talk it out with the dog. To get much-needed feedback, she just tapped its head and it nodded in agreement. Who needs a boyfriend when you've a got a nodding dog?

THE SWEET SMELL OF SUCCESS

Scientists have confirmed what the ancient Egyptians and Greeks knew thousands of years ago, that certain smells evoke certain behaviours. Dead obvious really: if you get a whiff of something off, you don't hang around to savour it. On the other hand, if the air is heavy with oooh-sooo lovely smells then you might settle down to enjoy them. The smell of rosemary is said to enhance memory; basil and bergamot can relieve pre-exam stress and increase concentration; and ylang-ylang, sandalwood and eucalyptus will stimulate even the dullest of grey cells. And when you're ready to relax, fill the air with camomile or patchouli. So, in the name of education, go out and buy some incense or scented oils. Your Homework Heaven

DID YOU KNOW EUCALYPTUS is SUPPOSED TO STIMULATE The DULLEST OF GREY CELLS?

will smell... heavenly, and the scent also repels parents, siblings and other gnats.

ARE THERE COMPUTERS IN HEAVEN?

Paradise doesn't necessarily mean having a computer. If your family can afford one, terrific. Even though a computer and printer will allow you to hand in beautiful-looking essays and projects (no mistakes, thanks to the spelling and grammar checker), a computer is only as good as the stuff you put into it. Feed it rubbish, and it will spit out rubbish. The all-singing, all-dancing CD-Rom encyclopedias and the rest are only tools, and, like books, are only as good as your researching skills. If your Homework Heaven hardwear does not run to a computer, then just make sure you get your fair share of time on the school's facilities.

The softwear

So you've found a corner to call your own. Now you need to stock it.

The two most important things you need are a homework diary and a year planner. Both are useful, but only if you go to the trouble of using them (see Chapter One). Now lash out with some cash and get your hands on:

pens
pencils
felt-tips
highlighters
sticky yellow thingummies
reams of recycled, tree-free
    paper (blank, ruled, and graph)
ring binders
file dividers
plastic folders

It's no use having a Homework Heaven, then doing your homework with a rapidly-dying pen on a scrappy bit of paper and filing it away in a Tesco's bag. Where's your sense of style?

You will also need:
stapler and staples
paper clips (big, small and
**   fluorescent)**
ruler
geometry set
erasers
ink eradicator
white correction fluid
hole punch
ink cartridges
sticky tape
sticky labels (plain and pre-printed
ones with cheeky messages)
calculator

THE REFERENCE SHELF

These are the sorts of reference books or CD-Roms you
will need:

- a dictionary – not one with pictures. You're getting too old
for those.
- an encyclopedia – either a multi-volume A to Z, or a single-
volume one divided into topics.
- a foreign-language dictionary – preferably in the language
you are doing at school.
- an up-to-date atlas – using the one your grandma got
when she topped geography in 1949 is just not good enough
- a thesaurus – great way to expand your vocabulary
- a guide to English language usage which will tell you
where to put commas, apostrophes and capital letters etc.

It would be wonderful to have, or be able to borrow
easily, a year book, a chronicle of the 20th century,
a biographical dictionary and a book of quotations. These
and hundreds of other really useful books can be found in
libraries, but there's nothing like actually having some of
the books within reach.

The headwear

This is absolutely nothing to do with fashionable toppers, and everything to do with topping up your attitude. Get this accessory right and you've got school, study and the meaning of life sussed. Yep, a positive attitude is far more important than personalized pen-holders and a 'yours exclusively' desk. Without the right headgear, studying will be a long, hard, boring chore.

"Slow down girl, what are you on about?"

It's simple, really. If you believe you can do something, then you're halfway to achieving it. For example, if you know you have the wherewithal to do algebra, you'll be xyzedding in a flash. But if you convince yourself that 'x' will always be an unknown, then there's no-way, no-how that you and 'x' will ever become a hot item.

If you've got negative attitude you're in a no-go zone and it's time to turn back, because you're going the wrong way.

"OK Kate, so that's positive attitude. What about self-esteem?"

If you respect yourself and are proud of your abilities, then you've got self-esteem. And as for motivation, this is the stuff that drives the dream machine. If you want to be an artist living in the hills above Florence, you will be motivated to do everything you can to make that dream come true.

Them-in-the-know say that bods who have definite goals do much better than those who don't. But the real show-stoppers are those who write down their goals. Every time they look at their dreams and ambitions, it gets the motivation going. No goals, no dreams, no motivation, no reason to get out of bed.

A CHAIN REACTION

Once you've got positive attitude happening, it's a chain reaction. Check out this flow chart:

SUCCESS Attitude = Goals × Self-Esteem × Motivation × Effort

The thing about success is that it's hermaphroditic – it breeds with itself to make lots more successes. A triumph in one thing, whether it be algebra or French verbs, usually encourages higher expectations and loads more self-esteem. The chain reaction just keeps on trucking, baby.

"So where do you get it?"

For a start you can put down that catalogue and close your purse. Everything you need, you've got. All you've got to do is nudge it into action.

To kick-start your positive attitude just remember what a hugely magnificent and lovable human being you are (you did put out the garbage last night without being asked, after all) and are therefore capable of doing anything you put your mind to.

To find your self-esteem, say with conviction: "I am a terrific person (OK, so I admit I do some mean acts occasionally but no one's perfect) and I deserve to give myself the best of everything." Repeat frequently – impossible to overdose.

Now this is when motivation comes in. Decide what you want to do – grand dreams are all well and good, but be easy on yourself and start with a modest, short-term goal. For example, next week you want to ace a science test. That's your goal and motivation. Dead simple, eh? Now hit the books.

"WHAT DO YOU GET WHEN YOU GET THE ATTITUDE?"
You can use your supernatural vibes to help you annihilate your Achilles' heels. An Achilles' heel is not a bit of fashion tread for your feet, but a subject which gives you grief.

Achilles was a hero in Homer's *The Iliad* and the story goes like this. Ach's mum wanted to make her son invulnerable and able to leap tall buildings in a single bound, so she took the boy down to the river Styx, held him by his heel and dipped him in the mythical river as any loving mother would. Sure Ach became a superman, but only as long as his enemies didn't attack his heel – the only part of his body not washed in the river. When the enemy sussed out Achilles' heel, they gave him a tight pair of chunky-heeled shoes and that was the end of Ach.

My Achilles' heel was maths. I was down on the teacher, a total flop at fractions, percentages and number patterns. The teacher despaired, until one day a wise old bod told me about pulling my attitude into line. Once I got it straight and believed that all this maths stuff was well and truly within my grasp, I applied a bit of effort and asked for help. Maths and me now get on like Kidman and Cruise.

Four tricks for knocking problems down to size

1. Turn mountains into molehills
Put your problem in an imaginary washing machine and run it through the shrink and spin cycle a few times. Watch it go round and round getting smaller and smaller with each revolution. When you remove it, your problem is reduced to the size of a G-string for a Polly Pocket. You now tower over your problem. See any reason why you can't beat it? Thought not.

2. Make cocktail sausages out of bangers
In the centre of a piece of blank paper write down the name of the menacing subject (the banger). Rule a box around it (we don't want it getting any bigger now, do we?). Then around this box write down those aspects of it that make it a nightmare – these are the cocktail sausages. For example, with algebra you might include the teacher (I certainly did), trigonometry, poor number work etc. Rate these in order of fear level: 1 for those that cause occasional nervous twinges; 2 for those that tie your stomach in knots; and 3 for the mega killer worries.

Work on the easiest ones first. What can you do to sort them out? Maybe you need to do extra work on these at home. Your teacher might be able to give you 15 minutes of one-to-one tutoring. There's even a chance that your best friend can help. Repeat for those words given a worry rating of 2.

By the time you get to the 3-star killer worries, some of them may have been solved already. But if any remain, you have to ask yourself whether you can solve them alone or need outside help (see page 124). By initiating the first step to solving a problem, you're upping your positive attitude. Congratulations! You are now empowered.

3. REPACKAGE IT

You've shrunk the blighter and broken your problem into handy bite-sized chunks but you're still unable to drag yourself to do anything about it. Why? Because the topic bores you senseless; there's a motivation deficiency. What you've got to do now is repackage it.

Take *Romeo and Juliet* to heart by substituting yourself into the role of Juliet and your current heart-throb as Romeo. Don't hold back – totally immerse yourself emotionally into the balcony scene; feel the frustration of scuppered luurve. By bringing a personal element into the play, you've repackaged it and dragged it out of dusty academia and into the real world.

You can use the same technique when looking at the culture and history of different countries. Forget about doing it in the third person unknown (they did, he did, she did), put yourself right in the middle of it and walk yourself through the country's landscape and history. It's a walk you'll never forget.

4. CONFRONT IT

Tell your problem in no uncertain terms that it's really not worth all the angst it's causing, and that it's time for it to meet its end. Let it know it's got only hours to live and had better knock itself into shape before dinner/your bath/*The X-Files*. You've given the problem its marching orders. You're a tower of strength who is going to stick to the deadline. No compromises, no negotiation and definitely no snacks. Go to it, tiger.

Answers to questions parents ask

"WHAT DID YOU DO AT SCHOOL TODAY DEAR?"
Give your parents a quick run-down on KS levels, ATs, NCTs, RoAs, NIAAs, CDT, GCSEs and SGs, and I'm sure they'll never bother you again.

"YOU CAN'T POSSIBLY WORK WITH ALL THIS RACKET!"
Research into the effect of music on studying is not conclusive and it depends, say them-in-the-know, on the attitude of the listener.

Do they think the music is distracting or is it just washing over them? The biggest concentration crusher is not music, but unfamiliar and unexpected loud discontinuous noises. Such as the kind produced by squabbling siblings and parents mowing the lawn or rehanging pictures in the next room.

"WHY DON'T YOU SIT AT A DESK LIKE A NORMAL PERSON?"
It's not where you do your homework that's important. The crucial stuff is being somewhere that is cosy and ensures you peace and quiet when you need it.

"HOW CAN YOU DO YOUR HOMEWORK AND WATCH TV AT THE SAME TIME?"
Let's face it, not all homework uses all your grey cells. Organizing your files or planning a project is perfect in-front-of-TV stuff. Reassure your parents that you'll do all the serious stuff away from the TV.

"WHY DON'T YOU GET UP EARLY AND STUDY?"
The best time to study is when you are in the mood and loaded with motivation. Some people, like moi, are just not morning children. Others are pretty useless once the sun gets low in the sky.

Be your own judge – you can tell when you're working well or wasting time. The only thing you can't do is work late and then expect to tie up the loose ends early the following morning. You'll be burning the candle at both ends. Ouch!

"YOU CAN'T WORK IN ALL THIS MESS. LET ME TIDY IT UP?"
There are absolutely no scientific studies to confirm or deny this one, most probably because scientists are messy beings. The only downside to working in a tip is finding things, but if you can put your hand to everything you need even though it is buried under a year's worth of *Just Seventeen* magazines, then don't worry. Parents have notoriously low mess thresholds and a stray piece of paper will send them racing for the vacuum cleaner. If you can live, work and find your favourite jumper, then your room's fine.

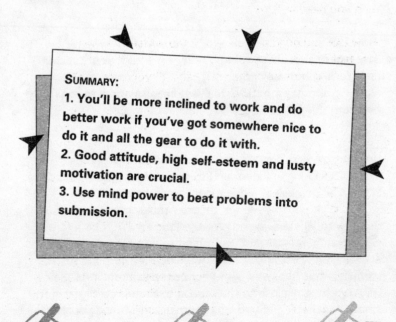

SUMMARY:
1. You'll be more inclined to work and do better work if you've got somewhere nice to do it and all the gear to do it with.
2. Good attitude, high self-esteem and lusty motivation are crucial.
3. Use mind power to beat problems into submission.

THE CLASS ACT

- Everything about: spending quality time with your teacher and making notes of note
- Nothing about: pathetic acts like giving an apple to the teacher

Howdy partners, time to get in the OK Corral Classroom. And just like breaking in a bucking bronco, getting on with the class act can be one hell of a ride for the unprepared.

You've got to have the tenacity (holding on like grim death with all your fingers) for the long haul. It'll be a four-year stretch at least and you'll need to be kitted out for any eventuality: short notice round-up exams or no-good russling varmints that run away with your concentration. Your ears will have to stay close to the ground to keep up with the shifty sheriff teachers, and you'll have to learn to brand your corral notes like the oldest cowhand in the business. Last but not least, you'll have to lasso your motivation and keep it on a tight rein. So saddle up girlies, it's time to hit the trail.

Being a student is a tough, dirty, no-pay job. But, like they say, someone's gotta do it. Boo hiss.

What to pack in your saddle-bags

All Calamity Janes this side of the Missouri have their own ideas about what should go in the ol' school saddle-bag. Some pack just one folder and then file everything into subject files when they get back to bunkhouse. Others are happy enough to lug separate folders to school everyday. It doesn't matter which system you choose, just make sure you regularly file your notes or are well-and-truly clued up on the timetable.

The head honcho at the ranch may also say you need: a maths pack consisting of natty little plastic bits that always get lost and a calculator. Occasionally you'll have to bring in the makings for food technology, and art and design.

The school usually supplies dictionaries and set text material, and may even issue a homework diary and notebooks. That only leaves you to bring in pencils, pens, rulers, loads of paper, PE kit and your stunning personality. Your bags are packed. Now it's time to start mentally wrangling.

Ssshhh! someone's listening

Go into every corral prepared: homework done and having read over the notes from the last lesson. Questions to ask? Do it sooner rather than later. If you're up to your pierced ears in earth science quicksand and more quicksand is thrown on top, it's adiós amigos. By the way, your mere presence in the corral is simply not enough; you have to listen!

INDISPUTABLE FACT NO.1:
Listening has nothing to do with those shell-like lobes on the side of your head.

↪ Hearing is about ears; listening is about turning on the brain. You don't have to be bunking off to miss a lesson. Just sit there and don't listen.

Strike a pose for learning

To help you listen, take notes. Once you've got a pencil in one hand taking notes and the other is steadying the paper, you can't twiddle your hair, clean your nails, pick your nose, pop a zit, or play ten green bottles.

INDISPUTABLE FACT NO. 2:
Teachers like to see your face.

↪ Face your teacher – it's polite and they smell a rat when they see the back of your head. Want to impress and show you're alive? Then occasionally change your expression from one of rapt interest to one of deep thought. It helps an awful lot if your eyes are open.

↪ To show mucho respect and undivided attention your body should also be turned toward the teacher.

✓ ✗ ✓ ✗ ✓ ✗ ✓ ✗ ✓ ✗ ✓ ✗ ✓ ✗

- Lips should be slightly upturned at the corners, as you would for a smile. Gives the impression that you're glad to be here sharing the wonders of volcanoes. A sneer is telling the teacher to 'eat socks'.
- Now for the legs. A bored person swings their legs back and forth, and wraps and unwraps them around chair legs. Thing to do is plant your feet on terra firma – the ground. Point your feet and knees in the direction of the teachers and, other than wriggling your toes to keep the circulation going, keep your feet still. Do this for 45-90 minutes ... ooops, have I said the wrong thing?
- Those with a strong constitution can turn to Chapter Four to find out all about their teacher's body.

INDISPUTABLE FACTS NOS. 3-9:

- Don't sit opposite your number one love god – this is bound to be a distraction.
- Don't sit next to Rosie Nosepicker, Lusty Pimplepopper or Constance Footshuffler.
- Use the seat and desk as they were intended, not as a makeshift recliner rocker with foot rest.
- Communicate. You know, like make with appropriate and timely vocal input.
- Get along with your classmates – it will make those 'team work' projects much easier.
- Every time you daydream in class, threaten to deny yourself some unbelievable pleasure. (Chocolate bar denial works for me.)
- To make sure you're on the ball, ask yourself if you know what the teacher is going on about. If you answer 'Battle of Hastings' and you're in a maths class, you've got a problem. You can kiss that chocolate bar goodbye. Tsk, tsk.

✓ ✗ ✓ ✗ ✓ ✗ ✓ ✗ ✓ ✗ ✓ ✗ ✓ ✗

Give the brain a break

Your brain is housed beneath your bob. It has two sides – an A side and a B side (left and right, really) and weighs about the same as a pair of size 5 Docs. If you really want to push scientific discovery to the limits, you could thickly spread the brain, as you would Marmite, to cover 21 slices of bread. Now wouldn't that be fun?

The brain looks like something you'd never want to eat, go out with, let alone snog, or want made into a brooch. It has the texture of tinned spaghetti set in jelly. (Wow, now that I think about it I did snog this guy once and I was still wiping my lips three weeks later. Yeuk.) If the brain was meant to be physically attractive – like an upturned nose and a dimple – it wouldn't have been hidden away under your skull.

The brain consists of grey matter (so called because it is grey) and white matter (so called because it is creamy-yellow – now that's scientific logic for you). Together the grey and white matter are called the cerebrum and are responsible for thought, memory, decision-making, creativity and imagination. The cerebrum also handles the input from your eyes, ears, skin, tongue and nose, and makes sense of it all.

INDISPUTABLE FACT NO. **10:**
The cerebrum is crucial. Take it to every class.

The brain is a recycling depot

In lots of books they talk about the brain being a computer, but I prefer to think of it as a recycling depot with a sanitation engineer.

Every day loads of junk (information and experiences) is dumped at the depot via any one of your senses. The pile is enormous (for example we have 12,376 thoughts a day) and it's the sanitation engineer's duty to put it into the correct skip.

If the junk is muddled together, the engineer has to spend heaps of time sorting it before storing. And while the junk is sitting there it rots and decays. If the sanitation engineer gets tired, then there's a chance the wrong stuff will end up in the wrong skip. But if the junk is delivered to the depot sorted, then the sanitation engineer simply puts everything quickly into the right skip. Hardly anything is lost.

When you're taking notes and thinking about what you're listening to, you're starting the sorting process. The brain can then get on with what it's best at: storage and retrieval. And you thought I was never going to get back to the topic of taking notes.

IT'S GOT TO BE THERE SOMEWHERE...

INDISPUTABLE FACT NO. 11:
Being able to take classy notes is one of the most important SASSs you can learn.

Notable notes

Once upon a time this tank-topped prof (yes, it was striped, knitted by his mother, and sat about an inch above the belt loops of his flared trousers) told me how to take perfect notes. And because you, dear readers, by having bought this book are supporting me in my campaign to keep Britain's natural treasures off the 'At Risk' register, I will tell you what Tank-Top told me.

TANK-TOP SAYS:
① Never try to take down every word the teacher says. First, unless you're a stenographer you'll never get it all. Second, taking it down verbatim is like tipping an unsorted pile of junk at the brain's door and will not get the hemispheres humming. And finally, word-for-word notes are not doing you any time-saving favours at revision time.
PS You'll get cramps in your hand.

② Take notes using your own words. They'll be easier to remember and if you don't understand something, you'll know the moment you try to write it down. Hand-out notes should also be rewritten in your own words. (Am I repeating myself or just trying to make a point?)

③ Don't panic if someone else is writing ten to the dozen. You're not missing a thing, but they have obviously missed out on reading this book. Be a love and lend them yours.

Dear Reader, Kate is totally out of order here. Much better for the future of the nation's youth if you get your friends to BUY their own copy.
(The Editor.)

④ Abbreviate and use symbols. See Abbreviations (on page 118) for a list of std abbrev and room for you to add your own.

⑤ Important words and phrases are called keywords. To make them leap out of the page underline them, put rules around them, surround them in stars, make them enormous, or do them in a different colour.

⑥ Convert words into pictures, cartoons, charts, diagrams or flow charts.

⑦ Don't take notes on what you already know.

Teacher-speak: telling the crucial stuff from time-waste waffle

Prick up your ears for these phrases. They are a sure sign that the teacher is delivering the goods.

To summarize
Most importantly
For the following reasons
This is significant
Bound to be in the exam
The main point
In conclusion
To simplify

To drive home the importance of a piece of information teachers will often use these dramatic tricks to get your attention:

- Repeat themselves
- Talk much slower and change the tone of their voice
- Move closer to you or radically change the way they are standing
- Pause and wait for everyone to look up
- Give a drum roll

SUMMARY:

1. Sit up. Sit still. Face the front. Teachers love it and you'll learn heaps.

2. Listening turns the brain on. Hearing doesn't.

3. Taking notes helps you concentrate and improves recall by a zillion per cent. What you forget can always be looked up in your notes. Cunning, eh?

4. In the wider world your notes are a record of what you have learnt. Your pristine and thorough notes could be your trump card in getting a job or a place on a course.

Chapter

Four

TO SIR AND MS WITH LURVE

- Everything about: the mysterious and unchartered territory of your teacher's mind and body
- Nothing about: your teacher being a total stranger

Teachers want to help, and an overwhelming majority care truly, madly, deeply about your happiness and success at school. The only zit on the horizon is that some teachers are better at the chalkface than others.

If you're an outgoing, outspoken example of the species, then a teacher who uses class discussion and debate as a way of getting the lesson's content across is going to score highly with you. But if you're the quiet, never-utter-a-word type, then these classes are going to rate lower than plucking nose hairs.

Whatever the teaching method, a good teacher knows how to get the best from the Gregarious Georgettes and the Silent Suzies. If your teacher is not doing this or committing other heinous crimes against studenthood, then it is up to you to do something about it.

This doesn't mean picketing the car park or rioting in religious studies, but you will have to speak out or put your gripe in writing.

Air your constructive criticism firstly to your parents (good sounding board against which to test the validity of your moan), then take it the teacher (if there is sufficient rapport between the two of you), or your year head, tutor, or school counsellor.

Getting a relationship going

It's irrelevant if your teacher is sporty, spotty, hip, happiness-personified or a hemline from hell, because what counts is how you relate to each other. If you get on, great. If you don't, then both of you will have to work on the relationship.

These are the sorts of relationship you can have with a teacher:

ON THE SAME WAVELENGTH – teacher/student relationship based on mutual thumbs-up respect and tolerance. Way to go!

TOTALLY ALIEN – neither of you has a clue where the other is from. Keep trying to find a common tongue.

BUSTING A GUT TO IMPRESS – both trying too hard to win the other's attention. Bad news all round: teacher won't be teaching, you won't be learning. Chill out.

IGNORANT BLISS – teacher and student exist in the same space, fulfilling their obligations, but rapport is zero. 'Who?' is the most likely response from both when the other is mentioned. As far as teacher/student relationships go, this is not the worst, but things could be a lot better.

BARELY DISGUISED CONTEMPT – teacher and student both have the distinct feeling that neither wants to be sharing air space with the other, now or ever.

What brings on this sorry state of affairs? It's like the problem of the chicken and the egg. Which comes first? Is it the teacher ignoring or slagging off the student, or is it the student doing no homework and making no attempt to contribute in class? A nasty situation that can only be solved by one or both giving in.

FEAR AND LOATHING IN LAST PERIOD – not the best basis upon which to build a caring/sharing relationship. Comes about when one gives the other a hard time.

New-to-the-game teachers have endless stories about students who have reduced them to tears. Teachers who have racked up millions of years of experience have even resorted to cosmetic surgery when students have laid into them about their appearance.

Most students have known that stomach-twisting sensation when put on the spot by the teacher from hell. I still break into a sweat recalling history classes with Miss Campbell. I loved history, but she could smell poor preparation, and chased it like a hound chases the fox. Truly ugly scenes. Can it be fixed? Yeah, but both have to come across with some praise and encouragement and be determined to give the other a fair chance.

TEACHER'S PET AND STUDENT CRUSHES – this is taking the whole relationship thing too far. If you have a crush on a teacher you'll be going starry-eyed when you should be concentrating. If teach has made you pet, they're doing you no favours by letting you get away with half-baked homework. Both parties have to get their act straight, pronto.

"Pray, kind author, what maketh a goodly teacher?"

THEY KNOW HOW TO UP YOUR INTEREST LEVEL. They inspire you, not make you perspire. An ace teacher will share the delights of charged particles using cut-outs of Keanu, Johnny Depp and Ryan Giggs. (Don't start without me, I'm on my way!) They will get you so involved in the ancient Greeks you'll be ordering feta cheese and olives for lunch.

THEY KNOW WHEN BOREDOM IS KNOCKING AT THE DOOR. A good teacher can sense intuitively when the first pair of eyes starts to glaze over and the owner is trying to remember when they last cut their toe-nails.

Superteacher will (a) immediately change tack, (b) get the class involved in something else, (c) own up to the fact that this material is heavy going and beseech the class to just hang in there for a few more minutes, or (d) will give an exhibition of six-ball juggling.

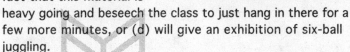

THEY WILL STICK TO THE SUBJECT. A teacher who's well-prepared doesn't waffle on about the combustion engine during a class on the poetry of Charles Causley. They will refrain from sharing the details of their evening meal and won't indulge in reminiscences about how things used to be in the good old days. You're up to your eyeballs in the reality of the here and now; you don't need their nostalgic baggage.

Every teacher tries to introduce other stuff into a lesson, but a good teacher uses it only to add a bit of life to a topic that's on its last legs. Digressions are great when used properly – lethal when not.

THEY DON'T MONOPOLIZE. Every teacher should guarantee you the chance to contribute in class. If you are being orally-annihilated non-stop for 45 minutes – heaven forbid it's a double period – then you're not getting a fair deal. Remind her or him that one of the cornerstones of the curriculum is learning AND practising communication skills.

A GOOD TEACHER KNOWS HOW TO PUT ON A SHOW. There is an endless supply of videos, games, books, pictures and resources that can be used to make the most demanding (read: potentially dull) subject almost fun. One of the best visual aids is a teacher with the watchability level of a Levis commercial. If your teacher is as exciting as watching paint dry, you gotta do something about it.

One of my uni tutors used to wear earrings the size of chandeliers, rings the size of golfballs and lurid knock-your-socks-off nail polish. I tell you now – you couldn't take your eyes off him. Gotcha!

THEY KNOW HOW TO OFFER UP A VARYING MENU OF DELIGHTS. The curriculum has made spicing up lessons with elements of other subjects almost mandatory. Not doing it is a hangable offence.

RATE YOUR TEACHER
Write the name of your teachers in the left hand boxes and then give them marks out of ten (10/10 is a perfect score) for each of the categories.

TEACHER	Showmanship	

A teacher can use poetry when doing rainforests; a Roman sculpture for working out volume; and for maths they can let you loose on the streets as a market researcher. As for cruising cyberspace and education software, there's just no stopping them.

A really good example of a mixed subject cocktail is in Gudrun Pausewang's book *Fall-out*. This story of a nuclear accident survivor (all make-believe, for sure ... I hope) combines elements of geography, environmental studies, science and English curricula. Sounds like a good deal to me: four subjects for the price of one.

If your teacher is not lashing out on the lively stuff, then she or he hasn't really got a handle on the curriculum, you poor dears.

THEY SET A GOOD EXAMPLE. Like you, teachers should be punctual, prepared, polite, and ready to listen. Most importantly, a good teacher will return homework and assignments promptly and provide helpful notes. Is your teacher up to scratch?

Willingness to listen	Waffle level	Piles on the praise	Dress sense	BO level

THEY ARE FULL OF PRAISE AND ENCOURAGEMENT. Teachers worth their salt know that the greatest return comes from singing praises for work well done. No one shines if they are made to look a fool or are constantly on the receiving end of put-downs. A good teacher will find your strengths and boost them.

1

THEY EMPOWER YOU. They don't give you the answers, but the tools for finding the answers.

2

Seven ways to rub a teacher up the wrong way

1. Answering every question with an 'um'. Won't work unless you're doing backing vocals for U2.

2. Treating them as if they (a) were never young, (b) are ignorant of the ways of the world, (c) have no life outside school, and (d) are hard of hearing.

3. Arriving late ... always.

3

4. Not turning in presentable work on time and then giving them an excuse that wouldn't wash in Persil.

5. Winding up other students. This is a really bad move.

6. Using your entire vocabulary of body language to say "I don't want to be here. School is cramping my style."

7. Picking on them. Teachers have feelings too, you know!

FLY GIRL!

Six things you won't tolerate from a teacher

1. **HARASSMENT** – persistently causing you grief for no good reason. For example, always picking on you for poor marks and late homework when you know there are other jerks in the class who do exactly the same as you.

2. ABUSE – physical abuse (being struck or shoved around), sexual assault (being touched, rubbed up against, or worse) and verbal abuse (shouting at you) are all big, big no-nos. Seek help NOW from an adult you trust.

3. DISCRIMINATION – if you think you are being treated differently or unfairly because of race, religion, ability or gender, tell your year tutor or school counsellor.

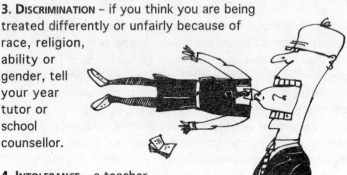

4. INTOLERANCE – a teacher cannot expect you to drop your beliefs and accept theirs. If you think your work is being marked down because you see things differently, your teacher is being intolerant. Time to speak out.

5. CHEATING – if you can believe anything that's written in the newspapers then cheating among teachers is becoming common. Some teachers are selling exam questions, doing their students' coursework, and giving early warning of exam questions. It's not on. If your teacher is into this, does he or she deserve to be your teacher? I doubt it.

6. FAVOURITISM – another form of discrimination, where one student is getting an easy ride (extra time for assignments, being given marks exceeding the work's worth, receiving extra attention) to the detriment of everyone else in the class.

Got a problem?

A good teacher will know if you're in a spot of personal or academic trouble. No matter how hard you try to keep it under wraps it will eventually show in your attitude, attendance, or standard of work. Teachers also have ears and no matter how discreet you or your friends are, they'll eventually hear something on the grapevine. And surprise, surprise, teachers talk to each other.

If it's a personal problem it's your decision whether you share it or not. But if it's going to affect your work, the quicker you spill the beans, the sooner a solution can be found.

If what you share with your teacher involves anything illegal (for example, drug or alcohol abuse, abuse at home) they are bound to pass that information on to the head. The head may pass that information on to the school governors, counsellor or the authorities. If you tell your teacher that you are pregnant, have an eating disorder or are being bullied, for example, the school will tell your parents.

There is a way to get help without setting off the alarm bells. Ask your teacher or counsellor to recommend someone who can give confidential advice. Just say it's for a friend.

"My teacher's got no heart!"

If your teacher is slow on the uptake, suffering from a compassion deficiency or hasn't clocked that you are in a serious academic bind, cut out and keep this Teacher Prompt Card. When you go to your teacher with a problem give them this card so that they know what to say.

Teacher Prompt Card
- ✎ I wonder how you are feeling?
- ✎ What is the problem?
- ✎ How do you feel about it?
- ✎ What are your options?
- ✎ How do you feel about each option?
- ✎ Which option will you choose?
- ✎ How are you going to put it into action?
- ✎ Can I or someone else help?

Is your school achieving its full potential?

Education and schooling are front-page news, and most of it bad. You know the sort of stuff: poor teaching, cheating, large class sizes, poor exam performances, declining resources, overworked teachers, and violence in the playground.

But whatever hassles are giving your headteacher headaches, your school has to give you a well-rounded education based on the National, Northern Ireland or Scottish Curricula. It has to make you exam and career-ready, give you lots of PE, RE and sex education, and offer subjects beyond the scope of the curriculum.

Ah, but there's more. A school should be a safe, bully-free and non-discriminatory environment. It should be a happy place where mutual respect and tolerance are encouraged; a place where you can achieve your full potential; a place where teachers draw smiley faces on your work and give you 'Excellent worker' stickers. No one can learn anything if their school is low on good times and high on hassles (see Help on page 124).

How to tell if your school is coping

1. There is no revolving door on the staff room – like the teachers stay for a long time.

2. No one hides when a parent walks through the door.

3. The staff are not techno-phobic – hiding the CD-ROM drive in a broom cupboard.

4. The head does not put 'Keep out: deadly infectious disease' signs out when the inspector is due.

5. Are you and your teachers getting enough of the laugh thing? Psychologists say that happy adults laugh six times a day, and happy kids 50 times a day.

Read them like a book

Miss Prim is standing at the front of the class. Her arms are folded tightly over her buttoned-up cardie. One foot is tapping out a steady beat. Her lips are pursed and her eyes dark and glowering. A deep V has formed between her eyebrows as though a glacier has slid off her forehead. She hasn't moved or spoken for five minutes. What do you do?

SCHOOL CURRICULUM

DID YOU LAUGH 50 TIMES TODAY?

DID I MISS A JOKE?

A) tell her the latest knock-knock joke

B) run for your life

If you chose 'B' then you've got body language sussed. Yes, you are multilingual and can read a persons' thoughts and mood by watching their face, feet and bits in between.

If Miss Prim suddenly said "Nice day isn't it?" you would know she was having you on. Body babble is telling you that this is going to be one lousy day. Miss Prim is miffed. And not like run-out-of-camomile-tea-in-the-staffroom miffed, but positively nuclear and likely to blow at any moment, scattering grief indiscriminately over a wide area. Gee, aren't you glad you've done your homework. You have done it, haven't you?

Here's a guide to the most popular body moves teachers make:

LEANING OVER THEIR DESK, WEIGHT ON CLENCHED HANDS, LONG HARD STARE ... *Beware. Your teacher's not about to tell you good news.*

LEANING OVER YOUR DESK ... *Your days are numbered.*

CROSSING THE INVISIBLE LINE BETWEEN THEIR SPACE AND YOURS ... *The teachers are telling you they are on your side. They want to be pals.*

ARMS BEHIND BACK ... *Confident that there is nothing you can do or say which will phase them.*

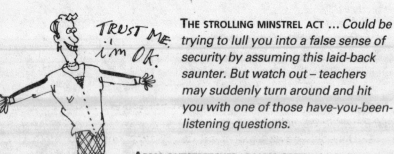

TRUST ME. i'm OK.

THE STROLLING MINSTREL ACT ... *Could be trying to lull you into a false sense of security by assuming this laid-back saunter. But watch out – teachers may suddenly turn around and hit you with one of those have-you-been-listening questions.*

ARMS OUTSTRETCHED, PALMS OPEN ... *Your teacher is saying I'm being open and frank with you. "Trust me, I'm OK."*

The problem page

Q   "My teachers go out of their way to make things easy for me. My legs might be in braces but I want to be treated just like the other kids."

A   The best solution is to tell your misguided teachers that they are discriminating against you. There's no reason in the world why you shouldn't be as miserable and stressed out as the next person in the class.

Q   "Our PE teacher thinks everyone is a Linford Christie, but I'm not. Why can't I just stay in the library?"

A   Poor you, you have my sympathy, but the law's the law. You've gotta get with the kit and get physical. Mind you the law doesn't say you have to be good at sport, just a participant. Suggest that your school expand its range of PE options to appeal to all levels of sporting inability.

Q   "In sex education classes the teacher goes on about stuff which is totally the opposite of what my parents teach me and believe. What do I do?"

A   Tell your parents or bring it to the attention of the school counsellor or year tutor. Your parents have the right to withdraw you from these classes. See Help on page 124.

Q   "Mr Greeves – though Mr Grief is a better name – has got it in for me."

A   Dig deep into your conscience to make sure you're not provoking his wrath. Maybe he feels you need this treatment to make you work to your potential. If not, then label all your work 'I respond well to kindness'.

Q   "I always put my hand up to answer questions, and not once have I been picked."

A   Lucky you! I never used to put up my hand, and I was always asked. Be grateful for small mercies.

Q *"The history mistress just rabbits on as if the class wasn't there."*

A In the middle of a waffle, ask the teacher if you should be taking notes and will any of this valuable information appear in an exam question. A little bit of tact goes a long way.

Q *"I'm really having trouble with French grammar and the teacher doesn't even realize."*

A Teachers are not psychic, nor do they have direct access to Mystic Meg, so it's up to you to speak up.

Q *"My assignment marks are always the same whether I do lots of work or hardly any. Is the teacher reading my stuff?"*

A Good teachers will usually make comments on your work unless they are severely pressed for time, or so pleased with your essay that mere words couldn't do it justice. If you're still worried I guess you'll just have to ask them. Easy, eh?

Q   *"I am terrified of my science teacher. Hours before a lesson I get butterflies. "*

A   There's always one teacher who will do it to you, so unless the teacher is giving you a big serving of undeserved grief, you'll just have to learn to relax.

Q   *"I think my teacher is racist. It's not that he's giving me bad marks, it's just the things he says in class."*

A   Tell your year tutor or school counsellor, if you don't think you can raise the issue with the teacher.

Q   *"Our art teacher is such a hunk! I go all goosepimply when I think about him."*

A   Forget about him. Lavish your attention on a more suitable suitor.

SUMMARY:

1. Teachers want to help. All you have to do is ask.

2. Caring/sharing teacher/student relationships are possible.

3. You have to make sure you are getting the best from your school.

Chapter
Five

AAAARGH!
HOMEWORK AND
RECKLESS RUTHS

- Everything about: grief-free homework and about the little known fact that kissing and reading have something in common
- Nothing about: burning the midnight oil

Reckless Ruth (surname withheld in case she comes around to Superglue my fringe to my glasses – again) was the form room radical. She refused to wear school-issue dark green bloomers, and wore G-strings or, as many of us suspected, no draught excluders at all. Sharon Stone had nothing on (ha, ha, privates joke) Reckless Ruth.

I was Ruth's groupie and a total sucker for every off-the-wall theory she had about life, love, lump-free yoghurt and homework. Ruth's Homework Conspiracy Theory went like this:

1. Homework is set by sadistic teachers who in a previous life pulled the gossamer wings off teeny-weeny insects. In this life they moved up the evolutionary chain to sap the life spirit of adolescents by heaping huge piles of homework in their backpacks.

2. Homework is designed to take up all the available time until the next lot of homework is given.

SEVEN HOMEWORK EXCUSES
(tried and tested by Kate) THAT DON'T WORK

✂ The gerbils made a nest with it.

✂ My mother thought it was a note for the milkman and put it out with the empties.

✂ A French mistral type of wind swept it out of my hands while I was revising on the way to school. (This one almost worked!)

✂ It was stolen by aliens.

✂ My astrological chart said that my homework star was in the descendancy, while that of *Eastenders* was rising.

✂ I had a nose bleed over it.

✂ I'm under too much stress and doing my homework would be bad for my long-term health profile.

3. Homework has no known benefits.

4. So complex is the nature of homework that humankind knows of no methods by which it can be reduced.

You can see why I was wowed by Reckless Ruth's argument. Her Homework Conspiracy Theory had given me four reasons for not doing any homework. At last I felt I was off the hard-shoulder of homework hell. No more all-night sessions doing homework. No more all-night sessions dreaming up excuses for not doing it.

Life was a steaming crock

Ruth told me I was doing the students of the world a favour by standing up for their right to live a homework-free life. But instead of feeling like the Evita Peron of the down-trodden, I felt life was a steaming crock.

School and home had become tabernacles of terror. I was earbashed for homework no-shows, made to catch-up during break, and my parents had imposed a sentence of solitary confinement on a ration of hassle, harangue and healthy food. I woke at night to the sound of my teeth grinding. Things were truly desperate. (Aesop-type moral fable coming up.)

I needed help, so I went to the library and wrapped my mitts around *Cutting Homework Down to Size*. Alleluia, I had at last found true liberation.

Test

The 'Am I stalling or what?' test

If you answer yes to any of the following then you have definitely pushed the 'Pause' button on homework. Do you:

1. think it would be fun to rearrange your sock drawer?

2. volunteer to wash, clear or iron anything?

3. think *Love in the Afternoon* or *Scooby Doo* would make for mentally stimulating viewing?

4. become wildly excited by the prospect of trimming the bristles on your toothbrush and pondering how they get stripes in toothpaste?

Cutting homework down to size

This trusty little tome said that all anyone had to do to cut homework in half was:

- Keep a homework diary and follow The Megatastic Grand Plan.
- Make sure you know what you have to do. Easy enough when the homework is "Maths exercises 1 to 10 on page 45", but not so easy when it's an essay or a mega project.

Don't be backward in coming forward, it said. Ask the teacher for the main points that have to be covered in the assignment. Which is the best book to use? How long should it be and how should it be presented? Can you do it with a pal?

If you don't get the drift the first time, get the teacher to run it by you again. Who wants to spend a week researching pig farming only to find out that the homework was Pygmalion? You need time-wasting set-backs like Joan of Arc needed firelighters.

- Get your priorities in order. Decide what has to be done tonight, what can be done tomorrow night, and what should be spread over a few nights or even weeks.

At this point the book went on to say that if you get these things right, you'll not only earn yourself more free time but more marks. Tee, hee, chuckle, chuckle, snort, snort.

Plan your homework according to mood. If you've had a bummer of a day, then start off with the easy stuff. If you've had a terrific day and are bursting with confidence, dive in at the deep end and do the grief homework. If you're into biorhythms – body talk at a deep level – then go with the flow.

- Only work in short bursts. Seventeen minute head-down sessions are ideal. Take a short walk or a do a couple of minutes exercise before you start again.
- Learn to be a good reader.

What a joke, I thought. This has nothing to do with me. Must be meant for some other sort of social inadequate. To prove that I was a good reader I kept on reading.

According to the book (which I had come to see as my truest friend) the ability to read is not coded into your DNA. You are not born with a library card clenched between your teeth and the comedies of Shakespeare tucked under your arm.

Yes, kissing is like reading

Reading is an acquired skill like snogging. The more you practise, the better you get. And you'll only do your practice if you're really enthused about what you're reading or kissing. The only difference between a bookworm (a hot lips) and a booksloth (a sloppy kisser) is practice, enthusiasm and technique.

Then it dawned on me that I was on to something that would save time in a big way. What you have to do is use the right reading technique for the right material.

SCAN THE MAN

Scanning is how you read a telephone book. You know what you are looking for, so you run your eyes down the page until you spot a familiar name or address.

Scan the Man is the one you call on when researching a topic using familiar or unfamiliar books. If you're doing an assignment on the causes of WW1 (note clever abbreviation); the key words you're looking for are: causes, Austria-Hungary, 1914, Sarajevo, Serb, Archduke Franz Ferdinand, assassinated, invasion, Belgium. When you spot these words, stop scanning and read the relevant paragraph.

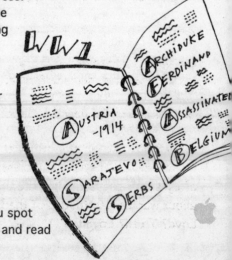

> Not sure of the keywords to look for? Scan the text for capital letters (which will indicate names and places) and numbers.

THE SKIMMER

The Skimmer reads the first paragraph of a chapter and the first sentence of each paragraph. If the paragraph looks interesting The Skimmer will read it thoroughly, or call in Scan the Man to spot the keywords.

SLO-MO

Slo-Mo is the only way to go when you're ploughing through technical stuff or set text books. You need to read these books word-for-word. Slo-Mo requires a lot of concentration, so go at it for short periods of time only.

THE PLEASURE SEEKER

When reading fiction the aim is to enjoy, enjoy, enjoy. Read at a pace that allows you to revel in the plot, get inside the characters and be swept hopelessly away by the blissful ebb and flow of words.

But because questions will be asked later, you have to read critically and know about things like:

♣ **Plot** – the order of events in the book that makes up the story

♣ **Genre** – what sort of story it is, for example fairy tale, horror, romance, science fiction, biography

♣ **Characters** and how they fit into the plot

♣ **Setting** – the location and time in which the story is set

The demanding English teacher may also ask you about the story's main message. Is there a moral to the story? Is it about wanton destruction of the Earth? Greed? Cruelty? Love? Truth? Loyalty?

Keep your eyes open to spot who is spinning the yarn. It may be the main character (first person narrative) or an outsider who is relating the story as though he or she is a fly on the wall (third person narrative).

If you are reading your own copy of a book you can use highlighters to mark important passages and descriptions. Use a different colour for each character or setting. If it's not your copy, make notes (with page references) on separate sheets of paper headed with the name of the character.

How does the author tell the story? If it's chronological or linear then the author tells it like it is. The book starts at the beginning of the story and finishes when the story is done. The opposite of a linear story is one that hops backwards and forwards in time.

To get the full drift of a novel, read two or three chapters at a sitting. Set texts should be read twice (you won't remember very much after the first reading), and try to finish the book in the shortest time possible so that you don't lose the plot.

Forget the hard way, take the short cut

Fingers blistered with turning over hundreds of pages? Eyes burning with tiredness? Have you ever thought of taking a short cut when trying to find exactly what you want in a book? No. Well read on, Macduff.

THE CONTENTS

This is usually one of those of pages you turn over quickly assuming it is just a piece of writer's waffle. Ah, but a good contents is like a good gig listings: it tells you what's on and where to find it. Forget thumbing every page, turn over a new leaf and use the contents.

THE INDEX

Tucked away at the back of the book, the index is the equivalent of a telephone book. Everyone and everything in the book is listed in alphabetical order; just run your finger across the column to find the page number where they live.

THE BIBLIOGRAPHY

This is simply a listing of the books used by the author to write the book. Tagged on to the end may be 'Recommended Reading' or 'Further Reading' lists that could save you prowling the library catalogues for other reference titles.

I was on homework's fast track. The hard shoulder was but a dim awful memory.

Always read anything in **Bold**, *Italics*, or CAPITALS and watch out for information preceded by ●●●●, ****, 1234 or ABCD. Don't skip diagrams and illustrations – they really do contain the nitty-gritty.

A good book (like this one) may start each chapter with an introduction that tells you what's coming. A summary at the end will tell you the most important points made. Isn't this book just the bee's knees?

The Six Rs and a W

(The 3Rs are for little kids)

This is how note-taking and reading fit together to make learning and revising-as-you-go easy. Your days of thinking that school was a chain gang full of people smarter than you are over.

Read – that's simple enough but make sure the brain has been turned on and you know what you're looking for. In other words: have you read the essay question?

Write – write down the important points.

Reinforce – read your notes to make sure they make sense and are complete.

Restructure – transform your notes using ideas in Notable Notes (chapter three) and Memory Motorway (Chapter Eight).

Revise – every so often go back to your notes and see if there is any way of making them more memorable.

Rehearse – mentally set yourself a couple of questions about the topic and see if you can answer them.

Re-read – if necessary re-read the original text to make sure that your own notes are still on the right track.

SUMMARY:

1. Cut homework down by knowing exactly what you have to do. Brain suck the teacher to find out.

2. The right reading method will save time, therefore your suffering will be over much quicker.

3. Getting both your reading and notes right in the first place will get you first class marks.

Chapter

Six

ESSAYS MADE EASY

- Everything about: writing essays that will have your teacher or examiner glued to their seat
- Nothing about: 'yes/no' answers

Look! Over the page! Is it a nerd? Is it a pain? No, it's PLAN MAN. With the super hero of organized prose on your side you will never again go into shock when confronted with an evil essay. From this day forward – and I can guarantee this – essay writing will be as easy as falling off a log (but not nearly so dangerous).

Yep, PLAN MAN is our top-to-toe essay specialist. One glance at his irresistible physique, and essay and creative writing excellence is at your fingertips. So OK, he isn't exactly David Chokachi, but how many times has good old Dave offered to help you with your homework, eh?

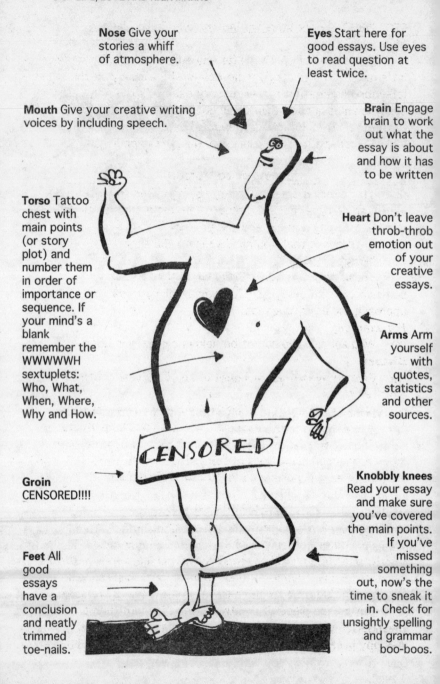

Nose Give your stories a whiff of atmosphere.

Eyes Start here for good essays. Use eyes to read question at least twice.

Mouth Give your creative writing voices by including speech.

Brain Engage brain to work out what the essay is about and how it has to be written

Torso Tattoo chest with main points (or story plot) and number them in order of importance or sequence. If your mind's a blank remember the WWWWWH sextuplets: Who, What, When, Where, Why and How.

Heart Don't leave throb-throb emotion out of your creative essays.

Arms Arm yourself with quotes, statistics and other sources.

CENSORED

Groin CENSORED!!!!

Knobbly knees Read your essay and make sure you've covered the main points. If you've missed something out, now's the time to sneak it in. Check for unsightly spelling and grammar boo-boos.

Feet All good essays have a conclusion and neatly trimmed toe-nails.

STOP PRESS: <u>Do not start writing until you have planned your essay.</u>

You can use PLAN MAN for any sort of essay, from the let's-get-the-facts-straight-no-opinion-here essay to the let-your-imagination-run-wild story essay. Put simply, an essay is an essay and they've all got to have a head (introduction), body (ideas supported by evidence, or a logical plot) and feet (conclusion or happy/sad ending).

Terms of confusion ✓

Sadly, for every moment of glory (being asked to write real world, adult-type 'essays' rather than 'little compositions') you have to pay a price, and the price of writing high-scoring essays is that you have to learn the lingo.

"What lingo?"

These are those dinky little words that appear somewhere in an essay question which tell you how to approach the essay question.

For example:

☞ Wild animals should not be held in captivity in zoos. **Discuss**.

☞ Give an **eyewitness account** of an oil spillage off the coast of Wales.

☞ **Narrate** the story of a day in the life of a head louse.

☞ Are *Mars Bars* more popular than *Kit Kats?* **Investigate**.

Those words picked out in bold are loaded with meaning, so if you non comprende le lingo of essays then it's the badlands for you. To save deportation turn to Terms of confusion.

The creative urge

Oh, it is a happy day when the only piece of homework is creative writing. For an hour or so you can let your mind wander over green fields and sandy beaches. You can relive the greatest (and worst) moments of your life, give shape to your dreams and slag off a few friends – all in the name of literature.

But an ace piece of creative writing is more than a meander down memory lane with the occasional full-stop. Ask any great writer and they'll tell you a ripping yarn is

10 per cent inspiration (a stonkingly good idea) and 90 per cent perspiration (writing it). To help you make the most of your cracking plot and keep the examiner on the edge of their seat, take heed of the words of the wise (that's me, in case you were wondering).

- Get your reader involved by using pronouns like 'us' and 'we' that invite them to join in the adventure.
- Pick a subject about which you feel strongly. Your enthusiasm and passion will be reflected in the story and dialogue (the talky bits), and will strike a chord with the reader.
- Don't start a story with: "In my dreams ..."
- Don't end a story with: "... and then I woke up."
- Don't rehash the latest cinema release or the video nasty you watched last weekend.

- When describing a character, do more than just give eye colour and hair length. Find what makes that character special and paint a vivid word-portrait. If a character has nothing going for it, does it belong in your story?
- Pull out all the stops and appeal to the senses. If your setting is the seaside, talk about the the salty air laden with the stench of rotting fish and the putrid pong of the diesel-engined fishing boats. This is obviously not a rehash of *Baywatch*, agree?
- Make the reader cry, laugh and occasionally snigger.
- Use all the tricks of language.

Simile: saying something is like something else. Similes have the words 'like' or 'as' in them, for example, 'Wield your words like a double-edged sword'.

Metaphor: describing someone or something using the characteristics of another object, for example, 'Our maths teacher is a dragon of the worst order'.

Alliteration: repeating the same initial letter or sound. 'Carmel is cool, calm and collected. Horace is one hunky handsome hulk'.

Onomatopoeia: making words from sounds, eg sizzle, guffaw, titter, sob, throb, phwoargh!

Rules are rules

Shakespeare ignored the rules of grammar and Jane Austen rode roughshod over the niceties of the Queen's English. But if YOU do the same, teachers will be down on you before you can get out an adjectival clause with an exclamation! If you try to flaunt the golden rules of grammar in an exam you'll be bidding a sad farewell to heaps of marks. So let's get with some golden grammar oldies and do a whistle-stop tour of full stops, commas and other wiggly bits of punctuation.

HOW TO WRITE FACTUAL ESSAYS WITHOUT BORING BITS

1. Keep the introduction short.

2. Teachers and examiners are looking for your ideas, so don't bore them by repeating slabs of text from reference books. Both teachers and examiners will have read it all before.

3. Don't waffle on about nothing, zero, zilch in the hope that the sheer weight of your essay will earn top marks. Teachers and examiners are wise to kids who make their writing enormous so that it takes up more room.

4. Don't repeat yourself. You're wasting time and it shows that your planning is up the spout.

5. Don't repeat yourself. You're wasting time and it shows that your planning is up the spout. Oooops

6. Unless the essay asks for your opinion, don't give it.

7. Use short sentences rather than long ones that go on and on using complicated or nonsensical punctuation,. –;! or absolutely no punctuation at all because these sentences will make no sense and by the time the teacher or examiner gets to the end of them they'll have completely forgotten what they're reading about and then ... Do you get my drift or did you lose the plot somewhere on line 2?

8. Make one point per sentence. Write about only one fact or idea per paragraph.

9. Put all the real mark-winning ideas toward the beginning – bound to get the teacher's and examiner's attention.

10. Use brief quotes whenever possible – it shows you've done the research. Always say who said it or where it came from.

11. Enliven and enrich your vocabulary, but whole-heartedly refrain from employing locution, the phonology of which you are ignorant. And now in simple English: spice up your essay but use familiar words rather than grand-sounding ones. If you don't know the meaning of a word, don't use it.

12. Proofread your essay and zap the boooooor-ing mistakes.

13. Do not sneak forgotten juicy titbits into the conclusion. Tsk, tsk, poor planning.

The golden oldies of grammar

Sentence: sentence starts with a big letter and ends with a full-stop, question mark, or exclamation. Somewhere between there must be a doing or being word (a verb). A paragraph is a collection of sentences (linked by idea or theme) which run one after the other. Aw shucks, there are lots of words used in sentences, but I'm trying to keep this simple. OK?

Verb: Verbs are either doing words ("I painted my nails a lurid pink") or being words ("Now my nails are perfect").

Stop press: The tense of a verb tells us if something has happened (past tense), is happening (present tense) or will happen (future tense).

Proper noun: This is a specific name given to a person, place or object. All proper nouns start with a capital letter.

Common noun: Not so-named because its behaviour is less than absolutely proper, but because common nouns are just everyday words and don't deserve a capital letter. For example: homework, teachers, examiners, school.

Abstract noun: These are for things that cannot be touched, sniffed, heard, seen or tasted. For example luurve, sadness, happiness and boredom.

Collective noun: This is a common noun given to describe a collection of objects or animals. For example: a murder of crows, a smack of jellyfish, a crash of rhinoceroses, a knot of toads. (These are all real examples of collective nouns and will earn you mega marks. Promise.)

Pronoun: A pronoun is used in place of a noun or proper noun. The singular pronouns are: I, you, he, she, it, me, mine, yours, his, hers, its. The plural pronouns are: we, you, they, us, them, ours, yours, theirs.

Adjectives: These are the luscious bits of language that describe nouns (**spunky** dude), possession (**my** boyfriend), quantity and number ("All **five** of us are going") and, last but not least, demonstrative adjectives that help you distinguish one thing from another ("I fancy the pants off **that** boy").

Comparative and superlative adjectives:
These words are easy to spot and use.

- *Adjective:* I am clever.
- *Comparative adjective:* I am cleverer.
- *Superlative adjective:* I am the cleverest. (And I won't have anyone disagreeing with me!)

Adverbs: Adverbs do exactly as their name suggests – they add information about the verb. Many adverbs can be quickly picked out from a crowded sentence by their -ly ending. Without the -ly ending they are just plain Jane adjectives.

Prepositions: These words tell us the position of an object or person. For example, across, over, into, past, under, up, in.

Articles: It is easy to get a handle on articles because there are only five of them, and here they are: a, an (used before a word starting with a vowel), the, any, some.

Singular: Use the singular form of a word when you only have one of something.

Plurals: Add -s or -es to words if there is more than one of anything. Like all rules, there are exceptions, for example, you can have one oasis but two oases (not oasises), and there is one formula but two formulae. The English language is littered with rule-breakers so tread cautiously and sleep with a dictionary.

STOP PRESS: If you use a plural don't forget that other words will change. For example: 'the band is on the stage' but 'the bands are on the stage'.

Punctuation pizzazz

● This is the strongest dot in the world with the power to stop a train of thought. A sentence just isn't a sentence without a full stop (or question mark or exclamation mark) at the end.

STOP PRESS: Use full stops in abundance. Examiners love short, pithy sentences.

❦ The attractive tadpole-shaped comma can be found swimming on the line in the middle of sentences. It separates phrases, clauses, and items in a list. Its main purpose in life is to make the meaning of a sentence crystal clear. When you see a comma it's time to take a tiny breather. **STOP PRESS:** The golden rule of commas: if in doubt, leave it out. Better still, simplify or shorten the sentence.

? Use this character when you want to ask a direct question. "Can I use a question mark here?" Most certainly! A question mark is an undesirable character at the end of an indirect question. For example: "Jenny was asking if you know when not to use a question mark."

! Shock, horror, gasp I need an exclamation mark! **STOP PRESS:** When you use a question or exclamation mark at the end of a sentence there is no need for a full stop.

❦ The apostrophe is a busy free-floating tadpole that stands-in for missing letters (it is=it's, they will=they'll) and is used to show possession. Not Exorcist-type possession (though putting an apostrophe in the right place can be a devil of a job) but the kind that shows to whom or what something belongs.

For example:

Heartbreak Times

STOP, THIEF!

Kate's boyfriend stolen by Jenny

JENNY and her BOYFRIENDS

SHOCK HORROR!! THAT JENNY'S STEALING MY BOYFRIEND!!!

Ⓐ

kate

Yep, that fiend Jenny took someone belonging to our Kate. Boo hiss, life sucks.

This apostrophe lark may look simple enough, but beware the plural noun. See the next installment of **Heartbreak Times** to find out where to put an apostrophe in a plural noun.

SAID BOYFRIEND NUMBER ONE -

Boyfriends' fury at Jenny's triple dating

When Jenny Rotten's three boyfriends discovered that she was playing the field there was no containing their anger. "We will all be dumping her for sure," said boyfriend number one. I know this is a gripping yarn, but did you stop to notice where the apostrophe was placed in the plural noun? Hint: look at the word *Boyfriends'*.

66 99 With cunning and guile known only to environmentalist avengers I have sneaked in an example of how to use quotation marks (inverted commas) in the above clipping from **Heartbreak Times**. Two head-down tadpoles go at the start of the speech, and two head-up taddies go at the end. Use a comma (or a question mark or exclamation when appropriate) inside the closing mark before attributing the speech. Finish the sentence with a full-stop.

To vary the dialogue menu you are going to offer up to your teachers and examiners, you can break a speech in the middle. For example:

"It's about time," said Kate sporting a mischievous grin, "that Jenny got what she deserves."

But have we, dear readers, seen the last of Jenny's appalling behaviour. Sadly, I think not.

Any questions?

How long should an essay be?

▼

It should be long enough to have answered the question. A good teacher will tell you what is expected in terms of length, but in an exam length depends on how many marks it is worth. The more marks it is worth, the more time you spend on it. For example: if an essay is worth 50 marks out of a possible 100 marks, then you should spend half of the exam time planning and writing it.

It takes me hours to research and write an essay at home. What's going to happen in an exam?

▼

By the time exams come around you'll have done all the research and revision, and you will also have put in some essay-writing practice. Pick a handful of topics and give yourself 30–40 minutes in which to plan and write an essay. If you get tired of writing essays, then concentrate on getting your essay planning down to a fine art. Works wonders for revision.

I never have any good ideas for stories. What can I do?

▼

What! Someone with your looks, charm and powerful personality has no story worth telling? Rubbish! Remember that time you were out with your mates and you tried to pass yourself off as a ten-year-old in order to get a cheap ticket, only to find that the love of your life was standing behind you in the queue? And what about the day you rescued those ducks trapped in the ice? No, girlie, you can't fool me. I know you've been places and done things that the rest of the world can only dream about.

I get halfway through an essay and suddenly realize that I've done it all wrong. What next?

Stop! Put down your pencil and don't pick it up again till you've read this. Your problems are obvious.
A) You didn't read the essay question thoroughly in the first place;
B) you didn't give yourself time to think about it and work out the best way to answer it; and
C) you didn't plan and therefore did not have PLAN MAN to help you. Don't let it happen again.

My speling is orful. Can you help?

Turn to page 119 of spelling nightmares and work your way down the list of spelling nightmares five or six words at a time. Divide a sheet of paper into five equal columns and head each column as shown below. Write your first five words in the LOOK column, and make sure you copy them correctly.

LOOK	COVER	SPELL	CHECK	SPELL
accidentally				
accommodation				
across				
achieve				
address				

Study each word in turn and learn the sounds (phonics) that make up the word and what the word looks like. If it helps, use the Memory Short-Cuts on page 119. Fold the paper over to COVER the word, then try to SPELL it. Unfold the paper and check your spelling against the correct one. Got it right? Give yourself a medal. Almost right? Then repeat the procedure and fill in the last SPELL column.

If you get it right second time round, move down the list and repeat the whole rigmarole again. Work your way through Spelling Nightmares and occasionally go back over the list and test yourself to make sure the correct spelling is well and truly loaded on to your hemisphere hardwear.

For spelling nightmares that won't go away try one of the Memory Motorway Tricks on page 99. Alternatively, just make sure you never use the offending word again.

SUMMARY:

1. Every essay has an introduction, a middle and an end.
2. A well-organized essay or story beats one that is full of ideas but totally muddled.
3. Improve your creative writing by employing all the tricks of language to appeal to your reader.
4. Good grammar, punctuation and spelling earn marks.

Chapter Seven

MOVE OVER BOOKS, I'VE GOT A LIFE TO LEAD

- Everything about: good fun, good nosh and good zzzzzs
- Nothing about: staying at home on Saturday night

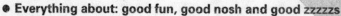

Want to revel in an orgy of thrills, spills and entertainment? Want to swap your books for some admiring looks? Then it's time to become a weekend warrior.

No, it isn't some incarnation of Mighty Morphs with a 48-hour fuse nor, heaven forbid, do you have to join the barmy army. A weekend warrior is someone who isn't worried about homework half-done and revision not done. Come Friday night they have switched off the desk lamp and are heading for the bright lights. Bless 'em, the world needs these angels with attitude in abundance.

Weekend warrior wannabes

Just in case you're not convinced that the life of the carefree weekend warrior is a highly desirable (and deserved) one, and you would rather spend your weekdays watching the vid and blowing the whole weekend catching up on school stuff, then run your eyes down this bevy of benefits.

1. You don't have to get home early in order to be up at the crack of dawn to cram.
2. You can spend all day in bed relaxing and will therefore be …
3. In top form for the next day of derring-do or classroom capers.
4. Your parents can't ground you because you've got work to do.
5. Interactions of the social, not alien, kind are important for your all-round development and give you the chance to wear all your fave frocks and earrings that dangle.
6. There's far more fun to be had on the weekends than on week nights. A quick squizz at the flick and gig guide in any old newspaper will prove this. But if you prefer reruns of *The Addams Family* to getting some Saturday teen spirit, then so be it.

There's also much more time on Saturdays and Sundays to pursue private passions: biking, football or shopping till you drop. Weekend warriors with The Megatastic Grand Plan get to hang out when the sun is high in the sky, the birds are singing and the living is easy.

Boffin attack

This chapter is also meant for those who spend ALL their time with their head buried in a book. You just can't do it. By hiding away you're denying the world your company. You have to get out and meet the common people, or you'll become a broom cupboard bod. Now that would be tragic.

It's not that socializing or in-line skating are the be-all and end-all, but they're good for your whole bod – they're like holistic. A good night out with friends or a day in the big outdoors exercises those parts that studying can't reach.

The more you experience, the more you laugh, and the more you get out of life. Need I say more ... again?

Job on the side

Did you know that over 40 per cent of 10–15 year olds have a job? Some are up with the sun to get paper rounds and milk runs done. Others, like babysitters, don't get home until the wee hours. But whatever dosh-earning lark you're into, there may come a time when it's all too much.

You might start skipping your homework or falling behind on a project. There may come a day when doing your job means there's no time to be a weekend warrior. What are you going to do?

A. Work till you drop

B. Find more hours in the day.

C. Work out a compromise.

A is a lousy idea, and **B** is a great idea but has no chance of success. The only way to go is **C**.

Short of chucking in your job, you could try job sharing. Sure you'll get less money, but what money you do earn you'll get a chance to enjoy. With your employer's approval get a like-minded friend to work alternate days and weeks, or to take over the whole job for a short time while you study.

Maybe your working hours could be reduced. A couple of extra hours a week for The Megatastic Grand Plan or for being a weekend warrior could make a big difference.

REMINDS me of SOMETHING...

EVERY thing UNDER £100.

Can your family help? It wouldn't be the first time that a paper round is done by a loving and concerned mum or dad.

Or is there another job with shorter or kinder hours that's just begging for your skills?

Ever thought of being self-employed? You can set your own hours, rates of pay and work conditions. Find a gap in the services sector of your neighbourhood. What about car cleaning, gardening, window washing, helping a family with a brood of kids, or shopping for old people? You could act as a recycling centre for your neighbourhood. You could collect everything on a regular basis for a small fee and with the gracious consent of your parents store it and then get it to the recycling centre every couple of weeks.

Millionaire status may not be around the corner, but at least you won't be a teenage burn-out.

Way to go, weekend warriors

Five-star ways for spending your weekend

★★★★★ Buy an Ordnance Survey map of your area and plot some half-day or all-day rides or walks you can do with friends. This is a good way to get in some geography map-reading practice, learn about your locality, and exercise all at the same time. Me, I'd also look for an ace café that makes a good hot chocolate with mountain-sized dollops of cream sprinkled with grated chocolate.

DON'T GET RIPPED OFF

1. If you're under 13 you can't work legally in a part-time job, but you can do casual jobs for neighbours.

2. If you're under 16 you can't be employed (regulations are different if you are working for your parents) in any kind of manual labour, nor can you work in factories, quarries, or on construction sites. You'll be pleased to know that heartless scrooges cannot send you up chimneys or down mines these days.

3. If you're under 15 you can't work more than 20 hours per week. This increases to 30 hours when you're 16.

4. Paper rounds and the like should be done between 7am–8am and 5pm–7pm. Any other job should not start before 7am, nor finish later 7pm.

5. There are no laws covering the minimum rates of pay for those under 16. Sorry.

★★★★★ In the foyer of your local library there are hundreds of brochures advertising all manner of courses, cultural events, cheap day trips and special-interest clubs.

The sort of stuff on offer in my local library were: lessons in baton-twirling, juggling, theatre arts, steel-band, belly-dancing, first aid, life-saving, and as many arts and crafts classes as any aspiring Rennie MacIntosh would ever want. There were also auditions for the local Am. Dram. Soc., a plea for volunteers to help clear the footpaths on the common, and a try-out session for the netball team.

A bus company was offering really cheap deals on day trips to Stonehenge, Dover or Oxford University (one can dream, can't one?) and a touring theatre company was giving a performance of *A Midsummer Night's Dream*.

★★★★★ Rock up early in the morning at your local leisure centre determined and equipped to spend the entire day wet, sweating, and on the move. Book in for a squash lesson or self-defence classes. In the evening many leisure centres, especially during the holidays, run discos. Voilà, your day is complete.

✭✭✭✭✭ Ask your parents to give over a small part of their garden so you can start an organic fruit, veg and herb plot. Other than a little outlay of cash for some seeds, seedlings and compost (the pongier the better), the rest can be stolen ... er, borrowed from your parents.

Expectations of the work a veg garden requires might initially put you off the idea, but your efforts will be rewarded when you toss your first home-grown salad and smother it with your own herb dressing. By the way, only anoraks have to tune in to *Gardener's Question Time*.

✭✭✭✭✭ Drag all your clothes out of your wardrobe and drawers and do the big sort. Those that don't make the grade can be bagged up for charity or given a make-over.

Unpick the sleeves off a skaggy long-sleeved shirt to wear over T-shirts; tizz up a plain jumper with tat from your jewellery box; cut-off your jeans to make shorts and to save on the needlework leave the edges frayed; or brew up a vat of hot-water dye and give your T-shirts and crop tops a new lease of life.

Even if you wear your own designer number only a handful of times, it's better than the original languishing in the nether regions of your wardrobe.

✭✭✭✭✭ Hit the museums, art galleries and any special exhibitions you can find. OK so it's sort of educational, but your parents will give the outings their blessing. There are bound to be few moments during your worthy adventures for a little shopping, eating, and socializing. Nod, nod, wink, wink.

✭✭✭✭✭ Get physical and try one of these: sailing, horse-riding, wall-climbing (abseiling follows naturally), in-line roller hockey (puck but no ice ruck), mountain biking, cross-country running (groups a must), tap dancing, jazz dance, badminton, synchronized swimming (don't smile – a nose clip makes you look like something served with chips), gymnastics, ice skating or tennis.

★★★★★ Go fly a kite.

★★★★★ Feed the spirit by gently immersing yourself in yoga, meditation, pottery, art classes, music, and bird watching.

★★★★★ Believe it or not, treating yourself takes time and it's important to make the time to do it.

Luxuriate in a scented bath and don't hold back on the loofah. Shave your legs and pits, push back your cuticles and buff your nails. Slap on a facial mask, put on your favourite music, lie back and put cucumber slices or cold tea bags over your eyes. Now relax and whatever you do don't get up to answer the phone. The cucumber slices or tea bags will slide down your face and bury themselves in your cleavage. But I haven't got a cleavage you say. Then they just go further. Mark my words, I know.

★★★★★ Don't just wait to be asked to go to a party, make one. No need to go overboard, nor for you (or your parents) to shoulder the responsibility for organizing it all. Divvy the jobs between friends – some can bring food, others drink, someone else can do the phoning around. At the end of the day your job might just be to give over your house as a venue. If loud music after nine o'clock's a problem, hire some dead scary, never-watch-alone videos, or use your imagination to come up with ideas for party games. I've never seen anyone say no to 'Spin the Bottle' or 'Postman's Knock'. Kissy, kissy.

The fit bit

To be a weekend warrior and a sassy sussed-up student, you've got to be mentally and physically on the ball. Scientists have proved that there is a direct correlation between health, attitude and performance. Poor health leads to poor attitude and performance.

What you've got to be is thrusting and dynamic. So how do you get it? You get plenty of sleep, enjoy a hearty well-balanced diet, and take some exercise.

Pillow talk

You need about eight and a half beautiful hours of kip a night. Sleep gives your bod a chance to carry out necessary repairs and maintenance, and for your brain to store, sort and bin the stimuli (serious word for stuff) it has received during the day.

Just as important as duration of sleep is getting your kip regularly. There's only damage to be done if you sleep 12 hours one night, four the next, and then sleep 16 hours to make up. The secret is in going to bed at a set time, and waking at a set time. If you do have a late one, then aim to rise and shine at your normal hour. Then your body clock has only been mucked up the once.

HINT: Power naps (10–20 minutes of shut-eye) are a big hit among overpaid executives who need to harness their stamina for a hard afternoon of paper-shuffling. So next time you're caught napping after last break just tell your teacher you're on a power nap. You'll still get hell, but you'll have the strength to cope with it.

To get yourself set up for quality zzzzs it's best to stick to some sort of relaxing time-for-bed routine. The worst thing you can do is go straight from a frenzied bout of book bashing to the duvet. Your poor old brain will be in turbocharged overdrive, when all it really wants to do is relax, wind-down and chill out. It's also best to avoid strenuous exercise and really hot baths before going to bed. All these do is cause you to toss, squirm and wriggle for the first couple of hours of sleep. You'll wake feeling like death.

So before you snuggle down, spend a little time doing something 'nice' (P.S. The thesaurus lists the following alternatives for 'nice': delightful, pleasure-giving, congenial, gratifying, satisfying, enjoyable, comforting and self-indulgent. If these words are inadequate try: hedonistic and sybaritic. But look up their meaning before using!); read a book of your own choice (not this one, far too stimulating and thought-provoking), listen to music, go through your face-cleansing routine or give yourself a gentle body rub with relaxing lavender-scented lotion. Packing your bag for school the next day counts as a wind-down activity. By packing your bag, you're mentally packing away work.

HINT: Don't change your sleep routine radically before an exam. Your body clock will be totally confused, causing you to nod off at the worst time.

HINT: Even after getting up, when your body has left the duvet behind, chances are that your brain is still in dreamland and will not start working at max until an hour later. So if you want to hit the books in the morning, be kind to your brain and start off with something easy. Your brain will thank you.

Sandman snacks

If you have to nibble before you go to bed, then try these sandman snacks which all contain the 100 per cent totally natural miracle sleep chemical, L-tryptophan: fresh or dried apricot, apple or peach; a peanut butter sandwich or a handful of unsalted nuts. For major munchies go for cottage cheese, tuna, egg, or cheese.

To wash down your sandman snack have milk or a herbal tea. Waiting for the kettle to boil and then watching the camomile tea bag seep is as relaxing as actually drinking it. Ahhhhh! I'm totally chilled. Night-night.

The nosh pit

What you need every day –

Naked vegetables: fresh tomatoes, carrots and green salad.

Funky fruit: as much as you like.

Powerful proteins: meat, fish, poultry, shellfish, liver, eggs, beans, peas, nuts, lentils, peanut butter (crunchy or smooth).

Cereal thrillers: wholemeal bread (and don't hold back on the butter or margarine), rice, oats, and ... er... cereal.

Dairy queens: cheese, yoghurt, milk (about 600ml).

H2O: doesn't matter how you get it but you need to drink about 1.5 litres of water a day.

What you need less of –

Cakes, biscuits, sweets, crisps, fast food, and tinned foods.

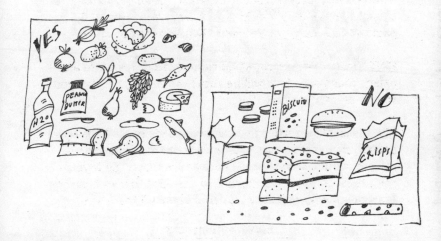

SUMMARY:

1. Everything, including school, is easier if you are happy and healthy.

2. Every day you need a generous serving of good fun, good nosh and mellow-down time.

Chapter
Eight

I WANT TO RIDE ON THE MEMORY MOTORWAY

- Everything about: memory techniques that are so hot they should be banned, and what the examiners say about your papers
- Nothing about: Aw, shucks I forget

An Avenue Anguish story by Zero Planner.

Honeysuckle Drive looked quiet enough but behind the door of number 10 things were desperate. The atmosphere was so tense you could cut it with knife. You could smell fear and taste panic. While the world was sleeping, Jenny was cramming. A whole year's work to learn, and only six hours left in which to do it.

Every square millimetre of floor was covered in handouts and unreadable notes. The bed was littered with unfinished homework sheets. Reference books were piled to the ceiling. The only evidence that Jenny had in fact eaten that day were the empty crisp packets and chocolate wrappers that had been tossed into the corners of her self-made hell.

As the church clock chimed three Jenny looked up, her eyes half-closed, her skin the colour of the dead. She had to keep going, she told herself. She had to memorize these boring chemical symbols and then play her French tape while she slept. Science and French exams were today.

Could she do it?

Jenny has stuffed this one up big time. Not only is she cramming (huge waste of time) but she's left herself with zero zap to cope with the actual exam. Things look grim, yet all she had to do was get her act together a bit earlier in the year and she'd have been snoozing, not swotting, at three in the morning. It's all too sad. I'm going to cry.

If Jenny had locked into The Megatastic Grand Plan this would never have happened. Her homework sheets would be complete and her notes and hand-outs organized and summarized. There would have been no need for hefty reference books – all their information would have been included in her notes – and the process of revision would have started long ago. She would also have known that eating well and getting zzzzs is dead important. Jenny's deathly pallor makes you wonder when she last saw daylight and filled her lungs with fresh air.

What Jenny had found was a sure-fire way to forget everything.

✖ Her notes were disorganized

✖ She was cramming. By trying to learn too many things at once not only will she forget most of it, but she'll get what them-in-the-know call 'interference'. Bits of human reproduction will be muddled up with conditions for decay, and chemical symbols will appear uninvited in her French comprehension. It all goes back to our stressed-out sanitation engineer at the recycling depot trying to quickly sort out a junk overload.

✖ She was rote learning. There was no chance she could memorize all the chemical symbols. You only remember information that you understand. Learning parrot fashion is for the birds.

✖ She was going to sleep-work her French vocabulary. Listening to tapes while you sleep simply doesn't work. Them-in-the-know have spent big researching this one. They recruited hundreds of hopefuls who were looking for the ultimate learn-as-you-sleep short cut, but at the end of each night the lazy learners could remember nothing.

✖ She wasn't interested.

✖ She won't remember anything because she never really knew it in the first place.

STUDYING – THE GOOD NEWS
1. If you're stuck inside no one will know you're having a bad hair day or are covered in zits.
2. You can lounge about in jim-jams.
3. No one will ask you to wash up/walk the dog/tidy your room.
4. Parents will pamper.
5. It can help you win the man of your dreams by pretending you're playing hard to get.
6. You skate through your exams.

How do you remember?

The better you understand a topic, the more you will remember. Understanding comes from:
1. Listening (with brain turned on) and taking notable notes.
2. Going over your notes frequently and revising regularly.
3. Getting any problems straightened out quickly.
4. Being interested in what you're learning. With a little imagination even Ohm's Law and logic gates can be fascinating.
5. Allowing plenty of time to learn.
6. Using all the tricks on the Memory Motorway.

"The Memory what?"

Motorway. It's the fast road to remembering dates, lists, names, hot telephone numbers and just about everything else you can imagine. You can even use the Memory Motorway to find those facts that are right on the tip of your tongue. Metaphorically speaking, of course.

You've seen those challenges on TV where a person is asked to remember a column of unfamiliar telephone numbers, and lo and behold after studying the list for five minutes, they can recite every single number.

Photographic memory, you say. No way – all they've done is learn a few tricks of the memory trade.

Oh, and by the way, you can forget about improving your memory by wearing a Daniel Boone-type beaver skin cap, drinking castor oil, and bathing your head in a camomile and laurel leaf brew. They won't help.

The Memory Motorway

ADVERTISE

Make billboard type signs to help you remember bits of information. Prominent sites only: inside the fridge, on the back of the loo door, on your mirror, over private parts on Keanu poster etc.

Good for: dates, spelling, language vocabulary, quotes, formulae, and geography (make wall-size maps loaded with detail).

ACRONYMS

It's easier to remember one word than a long list. To make an acronym take the first letter of each word and make a new word.

For example:

PATIA: world's oceans by size (Pacific, Atlantic, Indian, Arctic).

EATSME: levels in the atmosphere in order (Earth, Troposphere, Stratosphere, Mesosphere, Exosphere).

ROY G BIV: colours of the rainbow (red, orange, yellow, green, blue, indigo, violet).

MRS GREN: characteristics of living things (movement, reproduction, senses, growth, respiration, excretion, nutrition).

CATCHY PHRASES

Take the first letters of a list of words to form a snappy jingle.

For example: My very eager mate just spewed up nine pizzas. This stands for the planets of the solar system in order (Mercury, Venus, Earth, Mars, Jupiter, Saturn, Uranus, Neptune and Pluto).

Get the idea?

CHAT SHOW SPECIAL

Give Shakespeare the Oprah chat-show treatment. Find a friend (or a panel of guests if you're a power freak) and discuss the big issues of *A Midsummer Night's Dream,* for example. Should Hermia be forced to marry Demetrius against her will? Should she be free to marry Lysander? Just how far can parents push their children without a nasty backlash? And just how effective are today's conditioners and shampoos?

FLASH CARDS

Get some blank index cards and on one side write a word related to a topic. On the other side write everything you should know about that topic. Then you can test yourself or ask someone else to test you.

Flash cards give you three chances of learning: once when you are looking for information on the keywords, again when you are writing your flash cards, and yet again when you use them for revision.

Good for: foreign language vocabulary, historical events, geography and science.

KNOTTY CLUES

Tying a knot in your handkerchief isn't at the sharp end of memory technology, but it does make you remember something very specific.

Let's say your mind refuses point-blank to store or retrieve the formula for the circumference of a circle (2πr). Knot a friendship bracelet in three places (a knot for each part of the formula) and tie around the circumference of your wrist. When you're studying or in the exam you'll recall 2πr every time you catch a glimpse of your bracelet.

LEND ME YOUR EARS AND YOUR WALKMAN

Beg, borrow or buy a cassette player with record facility, and set about laying down educational-like tracks. You'll learn as you read through the material, and then again when you play it back.

If you don't picture yourself as a mic jockey, buy or borrow ready-made recordings. (Fast Forward's *Exambuster* tapes cover the curriculum and have been created by chief examiners. You're getting the good stuff straight from the horse's mouth.
No disrespect intended.)

Once you've clamped your headphones into place, you can learn as you go. Drive your family nuts by insisting that you play your rendition of *Julius Caesar* in the car. They'll never want you to go out with them ever again. Shucks.

Tapes are good for: foreign language comprehension, set texts, history (give it the BBC reporter-on-the-spot touch). If you need extra study skills or a confidence boost, there are tapes which can help, but get a recommendation from your teacher.

MUDDLED MEANINGS

The English language is full of words that either sound the same or look very similar, but have totally different meanings. The only way to unmuddle them is to make up wacky phrases.

For example: How can you tell the difference between

stalactites and stalagmites? Stalactites – tights hang down.
Stalagmites – mites crawl up. How do you tell your principal
from your principle? Easy. The numero uno at school, the
princi**pal**, is your **pal**.

NUMBER/WORD CODE

Before you can use the code you have to learn it, but once
impacted in your brain you'll find it dead handy for dates
(historical, not hot). What you do is turn a date into a picture
by substituting the numbers for its rhyming word equivalent.

1=bun, 2=shoe, 3=tree, 4=door, 5=hive, 6=bricks,
7=heaven, 8=gate, 9=wine and 10=hen.

For example: In 218 BC Hannibal and his pachyderms
were crossing the Alps into France, so by using the
number/word code we end up with an elephant wearing a
shoe (two) standing behind Hannibal who is throwing a hefty
bun (one) at a Frenchman standing behind a closed gate
(eight). History was never so easy nor so interesting.

Practise the code with these dates:

871 (Alfred became King of Wessex)
1643 (barometer invented by Torricelli)
1963 (Johnny Depp born)

OODLES OF DOODLES

Replace the verbiage with flow charts, spidergrams, bar
charts, pie charts, drawings and cartoons. Transforming the
information will make remembering a doodle doddle.

Good for: any subject or topic.

PRACTISE, PRACTISE, PRACTISE

There's no doubt about it, the more you do something the better (and quicker) you become at it. Remember when you first applied lipstick most of it ended up near your left ear? But now, because of practice, you can slap it on with your eyes shut whilst riding on the Alton Towers' corkscrew. See, practice makes for a perfect pout. So get your hands on some off-the-shelf revision books that are loaded with practical exercises to do.

Exam setters are also really hot on you going over past papers. These give you real world questions to answer and a chance to become familiar with how the paper is organized.

PICTURE THE PAGE

Make like Intelstat and, while orbiting over your pages of outstandingly glam notes (keywords all in mega-type) and diagrams, take a mental picture. Mid-exam, retrieve it and project it like a hologram in front of you. Just as good as having your notes with you.

RHYMES

How many nursery rhymes can you remember? Loads, I'm sure. Proof indeed that rhymes stick to your brain like chewing gum to shoes. All you have to do is make up short rhymes that tie together a couple of facts. Don't worry if your rhymes don't scan like a Shakespeare couplet, it's the thought that counts.

For example, days in the month:

Thirty days hath September
April, June and November.
All the rest have 31,
Except February which has 28 or 29 *blah, blah, blah.*

To remember when poor Anne Boleyn got the chop:
In fifteen hundred and thirty six,
Anne Boleyn was in a fix.

SIMPLIFY

If you really cannot get to grips with a topic and you've tried every which way to make it understandable, there is one more trick you can try. Forget your worthy tomes and head for the kiddies' section of the library. In a junior reference book you might just find a simple explanation to help you on your way.

SPEECH, SPEECH, SPEECH

Prepare a five-minute talk on a topic and present it to your parents. At the end give them a chance to ask questions. In an exam it is not enough just to know the answer, you also have to know how to present the answer.

Get some practice in with these knotty topics: logic gates (nasty, eh?), ancient Roman Senate, and the musical roots of Blur and Oasis. (Your parents will love it!)

TALL TALES

Create an off-the-wall story or film to help you remember an historical event or natural phenomenon. Fill your tales with celluloid and paperback heroes, and don't hold back on the special effects. The more absurd the plot, the easier it will be to remember.

Good for: history, geography and earth sciences.

TEACH IT

The best way for you to work out whether you know a subject or not is to teach it to someone else. Better still let your imagine roam and pretend to dazzle Patsy Kensit with your grasp of number planes, and bowl over Björk with a bit of reflective geometry.

AND SO THE TWO LITTLE PRINCES WERE DROPPED in a SLIMEY DUNGEON FULL OF RATS AND...

TIP OF THE TONGUE

Try these techniques to locate a piece of information which
has been dumped in the wrong skip: sounds like ... ;
looks like ... ; first letter is A, B, C etc; rhymes with ... ;
when did I learn about it?; what else do I know about it? You
can try poking out your tongue and studying it and, you
never know, this little diversion might just free-up the
answer. Still can't remember? Go on with the exam and try
again later.

WORD ASSOCIATION

Some words are hard to remember, so what you do is link
them to more familiar words or to an off-the-wall image.

For example: phalanges is the proper name for your
fingers and let's face it, it's not a word that pops up in
everyday conversation with your mates. ("Ooooh, I just love
that ring. It really suits your phalanges.") Instead think of
'fallen angels' and the word will come to mind as well as its
meaning.

Good for: foreign language vocabulary
and scientific jargon.

All about your exam papers

MEMO TO: *All Students*
FROM: *The Exam Marker*
Dear Students,
I have marked thousands of exam papers and I'm always
sad to see the same mistakes crop up every time. I don't
want you to lose marks so I've put together the following
list of common mistakes and how to correct them.
I hope you find it helpful.
Yours sincerely,
The Exam Marker.

Problem	Solution
Answering questions incorrectly	Carefully read all the instructions and questions at least twice.
Badly planned essays and answers.	Give yourself time to plan your answers and by all means scribble notes in the margin. Number the points in the order they appear in the essay.
Filling in answer boxes incorrectly, not filling in the right number of boxes, or leaving them blank.	If the instructions say put an 'X' in one or more answer boxes, do so and don't use any other symbol. Don't put an 'X' alongside the answer – it won't be counted. If you're not sure of the answer, never leave a blank, take a guess.
Wrong calculations.	Double-check all working out as you go and again at the end.
Using the wrong formula.	It happens a lot in maths and science. Before referring to the formulae included in the paper, work out for yourself which formula should be used, and double-check against those supplied.
Using the wrong unit (joules, metres etc), not using them at all, or forgetting the decimal point.	This is something you must remember to do. As a reminder, underline the units used in the question, and circle the decimal points.
Confusing the meaning of cause and effect.	Cause: cars cause pollution. Effect: pollution has an effect on trees
Only giving half an answer.	If you remember the WWWWWH sextuplets – Who, What, When, Where, Why and How – you won't go wrong.
Not using correct terminology.	Even though a science question, for example, is written using everyday words, to get full marks you have to use scientific terminology in your answer. For example, if asked what happens when water is boiled, don't write that the water disappears, say it evaporates.

PROBLEM	SOLUTION
Messy drawings and poor labels.	Take your time and do a rough in pencil. When you are satisfied, go over it again in pencil or pen. Make your labels easy to read, and use arrows to identify exactly what you're referring to.
Not giving enough detail.	You've got to pretend that your examiner knows nothing about the subject, and that you're his or her only source of enlightenment. For example, if a question wants you to list the factors affecting a baby's development in the womb, don't just write 'drinking', be specific and write 'drinking alcohol'.
Thinking that the examiner has no sense of humour.	Examiners like a laugh as much as the next person, so if you can make them laugh – and still answer the question – he or she will be eternally in your debt.

SOME PEOPLE HAVE NO SENSE OF HUMOUR!

EXAMINER

Six slick tricks

SLICK TRICK: How do you answer a multiple choice question? Tick every correct answer.

① By knowing the answer. (Well done, chucks.) ☐

② By taking an educated guess. ☐

③ By looking for clues in the questions and answers. (Very sneaky, Sherlock.) ☐

④ By eliminating those answers that are off-the-wall. ☐

⑤ By saying eeny-meeny-miny-mo. This gives you one chance of getting it right. ☐

You should have ticked all five boxes because they are all mark-scoring answers. It is a good idea to guess at the answer before reading the choices.

SLICK TRICK: Maths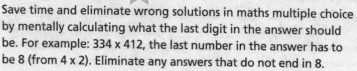

Save time and eliminate wrong solutions in maths multiple choice by mentally calculating what the last digit in the answer should be. For example: 334 x 412, the last number in the answer has to be 8 (from 4 x 2). Eliminate any answers that do not end in 8.

Other time savers: if the answer must have a decimal point or be in a particular unit of measurement, eliminate those answers that don't fit the bill.

SLICK TRICK: Comprehension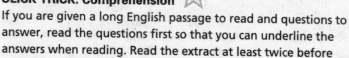

If you are given a long English passage to read and questions to answer, read the questions first so that you can underline the answers when reading. Read the extract at least twice before putting pen to paper.

SLICK TRICK: True or false

Carefully check all the small words because they could radically change the meaning, and beware of words like 'never' and 'always' – they are often used in false statements. Not that examiners are underhanded sly dogs but sometimes they make one part of a statement true and another part false. Nasty!

SLICK TRICK: Turn your papers over

The moment you turn your paper over and can start writing, jot down any formulae, dates, or names that are clogging the brain, stopping everything else coming out.

SLICK TRICK: Read it in the paper

If you can't spell a word or can't think of the right term, then quickly scan the exam paper – you never know, you might find it there!

Core facts

ENGLISH a b c

English exams are to find out if you can read (been doing it since Reception), write (no big deal) and communicate to your 'audience' effectively using words.

So, when marking, the examiners are looking at how well you write, organize your material, punctuate and spell. Never answer a question with a 'yes', 'no', or worse still, 'maybe' – the examiner will go ballistic. What they want are answers (written in your own words) that make a few points about the text or extract and are supported by quotes or examples.

In a piece of creative writing (for example, an eyewitness account, a newspaper story, a set of instructions or an opinion piece) they are really looking for your ideas, so whatever you do don't rehash last night's episode of *The X Files*, or end an essay with 'and then I woke up'. You may have woken up, but the examiner surely hasn't. Include descriptions of people, their characters and the place in which the story is set, and use a colourful and varied vocabulary. A story should have a beginning, middle and end.

SCIENCE $e = mc^2$

While your teacher is working out your assessment mark for science investigation, you have to sit an exam that covers life and living processes, materials and their uses, and physical processes.

Using ingenious questions, the examiners want you to show that you can use scientific terminology and use your scientific knowledge to solve problems. (Big downer on the way.) Them-in-the-know say that there are no short-cuts to studying science. It's more than a matter of applying your brain, you'd better apply your bum to a seat and get on with it.

Pay lots of attention to Ohm's Law, logic gates, using the right formula for the right problem, indicators and pH, word equations, chemical compounds, energy, and the conditions for decay. (Is there anything left in the syllabus?) Questions on these topics are usually poorly answered. You have been warned.

MATHS X = %

The good news: maths is one of those precious subjects that keeps going over old ground, so only revise the most recent work done in each topic. The bad news: the questions get harder as you go through the paper.

Them-in-the-know are adamant that you should attempt every question and do lots of practice on old test papers. You should show all your working out as they give marks for it even if your final answer is not 100 per cent right. Some formulae will be given on the paper, but make sure you know when to use them. Exam markers say there is lots of mark-losing confusion between Pythagoras' theorem and trigonometry formulae, and between area and circumference formulae. Squared numbers, square roots and fractions are other maths black holes into which marks disappear never to be seen again. Polish up on these topics till they shine.

Pre-exam stress busters

Take the dog for a walk. What, you haven't got a dog? Then put a lead on an obliging boyfriend. Ten minutes of exercise is the best antidote for brooding and worrying because it increases your heart rate and pushes the oxygen around the body at warp speed. Before you know it you'll feel like a new person.

Have a good sob. Crying releases the tension that's building up by ridding the bod of nasty downer chemicals.

Laugh. A hearty chortle lets the body's natural uppers run amok.

Talk about it. Unbottle your tension by talking about it with someone patient and understanding. Talking not enough? Go into the garden and scream loudly. Who cares if you frighten the neighbours half out of their wits?

Lash out. Treat yourself to really good food including lots of fruit, green vegetables, meat, fish and beans. If you're feeling lower than a snake's belly it could be because you're cheating your bod of vitamins B and C.

Rehearse success. Put all your exam fears in a bin, and then rehearse the perfect exam scenario. You're confident, the sun is shining, you know your stuff, hair looks great, your answers are just right and you had heaps of time in which to check over your paper.

Be realistic. Accept that you will do better in some subjects than in others.

Be cheeky. Blow a raspberry in the face of exams by saying (and really meaning it): "Exams are the not the be-all and end-all. I had a great life before my exams and I will have a great life after them."

SUMMARY:
1. Use The Megatastic Grand Plan and don't be a Jenny.
2. Follow exam instructions carefully and read questions at least twice and you won't waste marks.
3. Memory Motorway tricks work – use them.

Chapter Nine

THE ALPHABET OF EXAM-EASE

- ● **Everything about: life** – well, let's face it, once you've sat through your first exam, you've seen the scarier side of life
- ○ **Nothing about: being unable to cope**

Anxiety – Totally natural but totally undesired (like zits before a date). When anxiety (also called panic) sets in, take three deep breaths, sit up straight and say (silently, of course), "I am much too strong a person to let an attack of the itsy-bitsy killer worries get to me. Exams aren't worth the worry lines." See Killer Worries.

Assessments – kind way of keeping tabs on your progress. All the hard slog is done by the teachers.

Block tests – Minibeasts of the exam kind.

Bra – All important when it comes to exam comfort level. Don't want to spend half the exam salvaging shoulder straps from around your elbow, do you now?

Cereal – A must-have before an exam. For good measure also have a piece of fruit and a slice of toast. Lay off the diuretics like orange juice, coffee and tea (caffeine robs your body of iron, leading to slowed mental ability) unless you want to spend all your time in the loo. Just before you enter the exam room have an energy snack: banana, health bar, piece of choccie, or a wholemeal sarnie.

Dummy (I am a) – Four words that are never to pass your lips – ever.

Exams – Put simply and in perspective a three-hour exam represents only 0.0004 per cent of your life. Brushing and styling your hair, on the other hand, absorbs 4 per cent. Now is 0.0004 per cent really worth getting into a tizz over?

Failsville – A place to which you're not heading.

Grammar – Get it right and you pick up marks. The same applies to ~~speling~~ spelling.

Hairy moment – In every exam there is a fleeting hairy moment when you think you can't answer a question, are running a whisker behind time or your fringe falls over your eyes.

Don't panic! – Take a deep breath in through the nose, inflate your chest (does wonders for your sense of self-esteem) and let it out slooowly through your mouth. Quickly survey the room and admire the tasteful decor, and have an inner chuckle about the invigilator's choice of socks (and with those open-toe sandals, ghastly!). Refreshed and calm, re-read the question. You might have misunderstood it the first time round. Then you can a) tackle the question again, b) move on to the next question (carefully noting the number of the unanswered question so that you can go back to it later), c) mentally revise your time allocation, knowing that you'll save time on question 6 because it's dead-easy or d) request that the hairdresser in attendance comes quickly with Kirby grips. See, clever and beautiful at the same time.

Invigilator – the sorry soul who watches over you during an exam. And you thought trainspotters were history's only desperadoes requiring a life transfusion.

Justice – Don't let newspaper reports about overworked or incompetent exam markers stuffing it up worry you. Exam markers are extremely earnest about their work and they fully understand what you are going through. They are not out to cause you grief – they don't get paid enough to be that imaginative. Anyway, there are cross-checking systems aplenty, and both you and the school have a right to appeal if there has been an error in totalling the marks or if a change of level is likely upon re-marking.

Killer worries – A mythical affliction passed from student to student in the days prior to an exam. Intensive research shows that exam jjjjjjiiiiiittters are transmitted orally causing unnecessary stress levels among otherwise calm, level-headed bods. For killer worry immunity Doctor Keep Your Head says: do not share air-space with anxiety professionals and pretend total deafness (what you can't hear, can't hurt).

Lurve – A non-examinable subject which you may have neglected while studying. Catch up post-exam on some intensive passion.

Memory – Don't leave home without it.

Myths
1. Stress is good.
2. Quantity counts.
3. Examiners will know what I mean.
4. I can bluff it.
5. Examiners don't read everything.
6. Exams are the be-all and end-all.
7. Exams are all a matter of luck.
8. Long words and long sentences score marks.

Night before – After a bit of gentle revision, take a long soak while you plan something to send your family over the edge. Nothing like a little bit of mayhem to smash through the wall of tension.

Try a dead faint in the kitchen, glue your brother's favourite Pog to the sole of his shoe (he'll never find it), or take in your sister's uniform a couple of centimetres around the hips (stapler works a treat). They'll take revenge, you say. What! The night before an exam? Not likely.

Order your favourite nosh, and then before you go to bed pack everything you'll need for the next day and double-check you've set the alarm for the right time. What ever you do, don't cram, stay up late, or phone friends and cause an outbreak of the killer worries.

VERY DEEP WORRY LINES

MORE WORRY LINES

PARENTS BEFORE EXAMS !!

Parents – Poor dears will suffer *Examinitis sympatheticus* in the weeks leading up to your exams. Symptoms include: tetchiness, urge to nag and deep worry lines.

Parents will fill the fridge with comfort and succour foods, will offer to drive you to school, sharpen your pencils and sing you to sleep. They will need your assurance that everything is fine. Tell them that during exam-time parents should be seen and not heard.

Pee – Get one in before you enter the examination room.

Queen (Elizabeth II) – She also had to sit exams, albeit in a grander chair than the one you'll be sitting on.

Rubric – Not to be confused with the cube. This is a way-too-clever word for the instructions written on the front of an exam paper. Always read the instructions twice. Ignore rubrics at your peril!

Smug smirk – The look on someone's face when they finish a paper early and let everyone know it. Also known as Smug Suckers for not double-checking their answers, proof-reading their essays, and making sure they have answered the right number of questions.

Stress – This is something you leave at home. Stress affects your memory and concentration. For example: you're racing to get to the flicks and you're all stressed out because you can't get your hair to go the right way. You finally make it to the bus stop only to find that you're still wearing your slippers.

Time – You must know when your exam is, what time it starts, how long it is and how much time you should devote to each question or section of the paper. The more marks a question is worth, the more time it warrants.

Allow five minutes at the beginning to read the instructions and plan your strategy. Give yourself time to plan-out essay questions, and also time at the end to look over your paper. If you are running out of time and can't complete a question fully, list everything you would have covered.

Up chuck – A totally phantom desire to throw up all over your exam paper. Usually brought on by butterflies in six inch stilettos kicking the wall of your stomach. Even though a technicolour yawn might add to the overall drama of the occasion and get you out of doing the exam (short-term stay of sentence only), I can promise that you won't be sick. To deck the butterflies see Anxiety, Exams, Hairy moment, and Killer worries.

Vacant, vacuum, vacuous – From the Latin *vacare* or *vacuus* for empty which describes a freak exam state of mind. Moments before you turn over the paper you get the sensation that your brain has flushed itself, sending all your hard-earned knowledge to a sewerage processing plant. To reclaim misplaced bits of info you must first relax, then use one or more of the Memory Motorway Tricks on pages 99-105.

Writing – Tangible evidence of thought that exam markers look for. Good idea to make it easy to read, otherwise it'll all begobbeldygookandtheexammarkerwillthrowtheirhandsup indespair. Aaarghhhhh!

X – If the question says to put an X in the box against the correct answer, then that's what you do. Nothing could be easier.

Y am I doing this exam? – Because it is another small step toward dream fulfillment. Other possible answers include (cross out those which don't apply):

- delight in denying yourself endless days of gay abandon
- everyone else is doing it
- exam markers would be out of a job
- Kate would have no reason to write this book and earn the dosh to protect innocent forests. Do you want a flattened forest on your conscience?

ZZZZZZs – Get plenty in the nights before an exam. You'll need to be rested so that you can party-on once the nightmare is over.

SUMMARY:

Is there life after exams?
YES, so get on with it.

Chapter

Ten

LET IT RIP
REFERENCE SECTION

● **Everything about:** shorthand short-cuts, spelling nightmares, muddled meanings, terms of confusion used by teachers and examiners, getting help

○ **Nothing about:** taking the hard road

ABBREVIATIONS			
Also known as	**aka**	As soon as possible	**asap**
And	**&**	At	**@**
And others	**et al**	Because	**bcs**
And so on and so one	**etc**	Century	**C**
Approximately	**approx**	Change	**chg**
		Compare with	**cf**

Equal, same as, or is	=	Which	**wh/**
Not equal, different		With	**w/**
as chalk and cheese	≠	Without	**w/o**
Following	**ff**		
For example	**eg**		
From	**fr**	**MEASUREMENTS**	
Greater than	**>**	Celsius	**C**
Less than	**<**	Degrees	**°**
Increasing, or up	**^**	Grams	**g**
Decreasing, or down	**v**	Joule	**J**
Minus	**–**	Kilogram	**kg**
Multiply, or used to		Kilojoule	**kJ**
replace 'times',		Litre	**l**
as in 'He snogged		Metre	**m**
me 5x'	**x**	Millilitre	**ml**
Plus or and	**+**	Millimetre	**mm**
That is	**ie**	Per cent	**%**
Take note, girlie this		Per hour	**p/h**
is important. That's		Square	**sq**
why it's in capitals	**NB**	Tonne	**t**
Very	**v**	Watts	**W**

SPELLING NIGHTMARES These are the words we all (and that includes parents) love to get wrong. If you learn the correct spelling for five words each day you'll be through this lot in 15 days. Memory short-cuts are some pretty sneaking ways of remembering the correct spelling

CORRECT SPELLING	MEMORY SHORT-CUT
accidentally	**Ally** had an accident
accommodation	
achieve	I'm a **high** achiever
address	
always	**Al** always gets her way
already	**Al** has already gone
altogether	
awful	Looks awful with two ls

SPELLING SECTION

basically	Ally is pretty basic
believe	There's a **lie** in be**lie**ve
build	**Bu**nnies **bu**ild **bu**rrows
business	**Busi** business
calendar	It's got a **date**
colour	Col**our** world pink
column	
coming	

Colour

demonstration	
disastrous	It would be disastrous with an e
electrician	**Ian**, the electric**ian**
embarrassed	
exceed	
field	Find the field
fascinate	
fourth	
forty	U are not in your forties
government	
grammar	
guess	U guessed it

&

height	
heroes	
humorous	

imaginary	No need for e
intelligence	
lightning	Lightning strikes without an e
making	Making do without an e
many	**Many**'s the **man**
mischief	Good old **i** before **e**, except after **c** rule
necessary	**Nec**king is necessary
neither	Pronounce it 'ne-ither'
occasionally	
occurred	
often	We of**ten** go at **ten**
parallel	Parallel **l**s in the middle
parliament	**Liam** is in the middle of par**liam**ent
quiz	
receive	
rhythm	Kate's least favourite word. Please send Memory Short-Cut ideas to the Publisher.
safety	pronounce it 'saf-e-ty'
sincerely	**Rely** on since**rely**
straight	Dead stra**ight**, r**ight**?
temperature	Pronounce it 'temp-er-a-ture'
ultra violet	
unnecessary	Two **n**s and two **s**s
vicious	**Vici** is vicious
weird	We-ird!!!!
wholly	

friend

sincerely

SPELLING SECTION

MUDDLED MEANINGS

The English language is full of booby-trapped words – words which sound the same (or almost) but have totally different meanings.

affect	Something that moves or touches something else, for example, the ozone layer is affected by CFCs.
effect	The result of something happening, for example, the effect of CFCs on the ozone layer is catastrophic.
bought	Something you buy
brought	Something you **bring**
envelop	To surround
envelope	Something to put a stamp on
complement	Makes something **comple**te
compliment	Laying on a bit of praise (**I** compliment you)
hear	You **hear** with your **ear**s
here	In this place
its	Belonging to (This is **its** home)
it's	Abbreviation for 'it is'
knew	About being in the know
new	Something recently acquired
loose	Not tight or restrained
lose	To mislay something (You **lose** your **loose** change)
peace	War-free
piece	A portion (a **pie**ce of **pie**)
practice	A noun (I went to dance practice)
practise	A verb (I must practise my dance steps)
stationary	Not moving
stationery	Writing materials (envelopes are station**ery**)
their	Belonging to someone (**heir** to **their** fortune)
there	A place (**here** and t**here**)

to	Indicates an action (I go **to** bed)
too	As well (I want to go bed **too**)
two	As in 1 + 1 = 2 (now there are two in the bed)
wear	You **wear ear** rings
where	A place (**here** is **where** I live)
weather	Atmospheric happenings
whether	All about doubt and choice (I don't care **whether** the **weather** is good or bad)
your	Belonging to someone (**your** hat)
you're	Abbreviation of 'you are' (**You're** (You are) a lunatic!)

wear ear

TERMS OF CONFUSION

Calculate	Work out the answer.
Causes of ...	Write about the actions that made an event occur. For example: What are the causes of onion-skin weathering?
Comment on	Room for a bit of opinion here, but always support your ideas with evidence or examples.
Compare	Find the similarities and differences.
Contrast	Find just the differences.
Define	Give the meaning.
Describe	'Paint' a verbal picture. For maths and science describe what you would do to solve a problem.
Discuss	Write about a subject using argument, opinion and fact.
Effect of ...	Write about the results of an event. For example: What are the effects of onion-skin weathering on rocks?
Estimate	Approximate answer, no need to work out exact value or solution.

TEACHER SPEAK

Explain	Make the meaning or purpose of something crystal clear so that any dummy would understand. In maths or science the question may be asking you to say why something works.
Identify	Clearly name all the relevant items. For example: Identify which part of the ear is responsible for collecting sound.
Illustrate	Use examples to explain something. For example: Illustrate the uses of electricity. (Don't draw anything unless asked.)
Investigate	Make like Sherlock leaving no stone unturned and providing plenty of proof until the truth is revealed. For example: Investigate the possibility that doing homework is a good idea.
Narrate	Tell the story.
Predict	Suggest what might happen.
Prove	Use lots of evidence to show the statement is valid. For example: Prove that rain falls from the sky.
Summarize	Give the main points or tell the story as concisely as possible.
Trace	Tell the history of a subject in chronological order. For example: Trace the formation of an island.
Write an account	Tell the story.

Help

ALCOHOL, SMOKING AND DRUGS AT SCHOOL ←≪

Surprise, surprise but these are a big no-no on school grounds. If the school catches you doing anything illegal they can call in the law and expel you. The law will take a dim view of your behaviour if it has anything to do with illegal drugs, but the people they really want are the pushers.

If you need help or know someone who does, contact Childline (Freephone 0800 1111) or the National Drugs helpline (0800 776600).

BULLYING ✳

1. Tell an adult you trust.
2. Tell yourself you don't deserved to be bullied, it's not your fault.
3. Get a bit of class action going – 'SAY NO TO BULLYING'.
4. Stay in a group. There's safety is in numbers, so avoid being alone anywhere.
5. Instead of looking upset, look assertive and walk quickly and confidently away from the bullies.
6. If in danger – DON'T HANG AROUND, GET GOING FAST.
7. If bullies take something of yours, don't fight to get it back. Walk away and tell an adult.
8. If you think fighting back is the only way out – speak to an adult and let them know your feelings.
9. If you are being bullied because you are different, be proud of your differences.
10. Don't hit back.
    If you can't find someone to talk to at school, call Childline (Freephone 0800 1111).

BUNKING OFF ☎

If you bunk off because you think it would be fun to spend a day hanging around a shopping mall, you're a sad person. But if you truant because there are problems at home, can't cope with the pressure at school or just don't like school, do yourself a favour and have a chat with the school counsellor or other teacher-type person you trust. Something good is bound to come of it. If you're dead set against the school lark or think you have something better to do, the law says you have to bide your time until you're 16.

CAN'T KEEP UP ✳

If you are falling behind and your teacher is unable to give you any more support, try private or group coaching.

Admittedly you will have to pay for all this special coaching, but having a teacher all to yourself might be invaluable.

To find a good one ask for recommendations and look for the following gobbledegook after their name: CertEd or BEd, or a BA/BSc followed by PGCE.

Let your teacher know what you're doing, she or he may even be able to jot down a list of your weaknesses to guide your tutor.

DYSLEXIA ✗

There are about 300,000 children in the UK (that's about one per class) who are severely dyslexic. Dyslexia does not affect general intelligence, but causes difficulty in reading, spelling, writing and numeracy. People who are dyslexic often excel in creative subjects.

Famous peeps who happen to be dyslexic: Leonardo da Vinci, Albert Einstein, Michael Heseltine, Tom Cruise, Cher, journalist Nigel Dempster, and photographer David Bailey.

Contact the Dyslexia Institute (01784 463851), or the British Dyslexia Association helpline (01734 668271).

PARENT EVENINGS

The occasion when parents are more anxious than you. Tee hee.

PROBLEMS AT HOME

Head straight to your school counsellor for advice or referral. Do not pass up the opportunity to lighten your load. Do not collect more problems by holding back. Do not forget there's always a willing listener at Childline (Freephone 0800 1111).

RELIGIOUS EDUCATION †

Schools adhere to guidelines established by their local education authority, and a summary will be contained in the school prospectus. Parents have the right to withdraw you from RE classes on the grounds of religious belief. Parents must write to the head requesting the withdrawal of their child.

RoAs

Records of Achievement reveal the things that exams can't. Most importantly they let you talk about yourself.

SCHOOL REPORTS

Their main purpose is to exhaust teachers, as well as terrifying students and their parents.

SEX EDUCATION

Learning about the biological facts of reproduction – how babies are made and how they grow – is a compulsory part of the secondary curriculum. Parents cannot withdraw you from these classes.

Your parents can withdraw you from specific sex education classes that cover, for example, AIDS, sexually transmitted diseases, and contraception. (In Scotland sex education is not compulsory, but is taught in most schools.)

In their prospectus details, schools usually include details about what they will cover in sex education classes and what the classes will be taught. Parents may be asked to sign a letter giving their permission for their child to attend sex education classes.

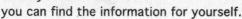

If your parents won't allow you to attend these classes, teachers have the right to let you know where you can find the information for yourself.

SPECIAL NEEDS

All schools must have a Special Needs Coordinator and a policy to help the one in five children who need extra support. If you have been given a statement, you have been given the legal right to special needs help. If a statement has not been granted by the local education authority and no satisfactory arrangements can be made with the school, you and your parents can go to a Special Educational Needs Tribunal. For information about appeals, contact the Advisory Centre for Education helpline (0171 3548321) or your local education authority.

WORK EXPERIENCE

By the time you are 16 you should have done at least one week's work experience. There is also a possibility that a similar program for disenchanted 14 and 15-year-olds will be started.

Some schools also offer Pre-vocational Studies (PVS) which are the equivalent of two GCSE or Standard Grade options, and are specifically aimed at students who would have difficulty achieving exam standard. PVSs are intended to equip you with job-related skills.